Blind Trust

A Story of Adventurous Dreams
and
Triumphs Over Adversity

Cover, map & drawing by Joanne Oviatt

Alternate Title, "Double Trust"

Copyright © 1993 by Barbara N. Ekey

This book has been printed in large type to accommodate the visually challenged.

Published by A. D. Clarke Publishers, 1995

ISBN 1-886755-08-6

Library of Congress Number Pending

Blind Trust

By

Barbara N. Ekey

A. D. Clarke Publishers

This book is Dedicated

To

Marty J. Phelps

Acknowledgments

Many thanks to the following friends and family: Jeffrey Hileman, Joanne Oviatt, Kay McCauley, Daryl Miller, Dr. Frances Lamberts, Richard Peltz, William F. Clinger, Robert C. Ekey, Kimberly Anne Ekey and Robert C. Ekey Jr. and numerous others.

Contents

Football Field
19,600

Summit
20,320

Denali Pass
18,200

17,200

Headwall

Windy Corners
13,200

Kahiltna Pass
10,320

Motorcycle Hill
11,500

Kahiltna Glacier

Mount McKinley - West Buttress Route

Joni Phelps

Chapter One

"The steps of faith fall on the seeming void, but find the rock beneath."   Whittier

BOUND BY FAITH

With the sudden tightening of the bright yellow and green ropes that bound them together, twins Mike and Marty Phelps felt their mother plunge five feet into the 900-foot crevasse before the safety lines stopped her fall with a jerk. The tug of the impact and the pull of her 140-pound body lent physical emphasis to the psychological wrench of her predicament inside the gaping maw of the crevasse that awed veteran climbers called "Jaws." All three, despite their tight-lipped, outwardly unemotional demeanor, were terrified.

As the climbers had rehearsed, 54-year-old Joni Phelps dug into the icy wall with spiked crampons strapped to her insulated boots and quickly drove her ice ax into a small crevice. Muscular, 6-foot 2-inch Marty, who had been following behind, immediately hammered ice screws into the ledge and side wall to secure her position as his identical brother, Mike, moved from his place several steps in the lead to lift his mother back onto the narrow walkway.

Not a word was said as the panting, heavily-clad adventurers paused a moment to recover at this fateful spot less than 2 miles from the summit of Mt. McKinley, but the trio knew they must turn back. Eight days into their assault on North America's highest peak, Joni was exhausted, plagued by diarrhea and in danger of frostbite from the need to repeatedly stop along the way and bare herself to the brutal winds and temperatures that seldom warmed above freezing. Though it was springtime in the world below, winter never retracted its icy talons in McKinley's unforgiving upper reaches.

The unspoken decision to abandon the climb reflected an agreement made before starting the challenge: If one of them was not able to make the summit, all three would turn back. It was heartbreaking but necessary.

Joni Phelps, a shy homemaker with the steely spirit of an adventurer, was on what for her was a religious pilgrimage, reaching closer to the heavens by climbing the mountain Native Americans knew as Denali, or "Great One," a name akin to those she knew for her God. She had had her heart set for the last 16 months on this most difficult challenge of her life.

The summit goal, incredibly treacherous by any measure, was made even more so by Joni's reliance throughout the climb on her sons' step-by-step directions. "Take two baby steps forward and then a big giant step," they patiently instructed her. "Keep your weight balanced."

She depended on their instructions as a physical manifestation of God's guidance. Since her teen-age years, she had sensed this powerful force guiding her life along the path of Christian virtues. She had led her sons to know this power, and now it was their turn to lead her up Mount McKinley.

Her hopes of triumphing over the mountain's bottomless crevasses, whiteouts and hazardous slopes hinged on the mental and physical strength with which she had been blessed. The ropes connecting her to her sons were not constraints, but sources of freedom, like the tenants of her faith that kept her on life's figurative path. "I loved the freedom the ropes provided me," Joni said with a broad smile. "I could climb knowing that I had this attached safety."

Quite aware that 11 people had perished on McKinley the year before, Joni had approached the climb expecting to test her acute sense of touch and hearing, keen awareness of her body and the knowledge of the mountain memorized from tapes made by her sons. She knew temperatures on McKinley can drop to a minus 140-degrees and understood the affects of altitude sickness, the dizziness and extreme headaches caused by low blood oxygen levels which could fog climber's thinking, making an accident more likely to occur.

But even more, she lived by faith and not by sight, trusting in her 29-year-old sons' common sense, their spare but descriptive verbiage, and extensive adventure training. She knew that their twin 190-pound bodies had met the challenges of high school and college football and had continued to grow stronger through years of competitive running, hunting and fishing. Her confidence that their brawn was equal to the physical rigors of the ascent was as unshakable as her faith.

Special Insight

Though most people found it difficult to distinguish one of the handsome, dark-haired men from the other visually and vocally, their mother had come to know them well through infancy to adulthood and recognized that they had matured into two very distinct personalities, two sides of the same coin. Outward physical appearances were of no concern to Joni, who had lost her sight 20 years before. What made the difference was the inner-self revealed by actions and words.

She took little in life for granted, so everything took on added meaning and importance. Though sometimes fooled, her special vision eventually "saw" the essence in people and events. She firmly believed that each day is a mile climbed toward being at home with the Lord in heaven. "My children also have a strong faith," she'd say with pride.

Mike Phelps, a control room operator on the Alaskan pipeline, had earned the nickname "Chairman of the Boards" with his determination, knowledge and ability to get rebounds during the company's basketball games. "Most of the time," she observed, "Mike's the one to make the final decision for the pair."

His older sister Judy believed that his dominance carried over into other aspects of his life. In fact, she noted, the 'chairman of the board' could just as easily have referred to the fact that Mike negotiated for the pair. "He was the one who bought the lumber for their house," she observed.

"He knew what they wanted and what they could afford to pay," added their pragmatic mother. In contrast, Marty was master builder both literally and figuratively. He had earned teaching certification before his love of the outdoors drew him into work as a self-employed carpenter and apprentice hunting guide. His thoughtful and gentle temperament was shown in that he decided not to join the National Rifle Association. Throughout the months of preparation for the climb, he patiently explained concepts and situations to his mother.

"Mom, each time you step on the rope, it damages it just a little, and we may need it later on," he'd say, concerned that a weakened rope, like the thin string on a

15

marionette would break with one or two powerful snaps; he did not want to be the puppeteer responsible for sending his mother to her death. Such concerns seldom found a voice as he joked and couched his descriptions in colorful terms, many of them drawn from his gridiron days. "It's a football field away, Mom," or "Ten yards to go."

To Joni's way of viewing things, Marty was the sensitive, creative one who had designed the log home the twins were building of Sitka spruce, the state tree of Alaska. His meticulous pencil drawings outlined his vision for the dwelling in great detail.

The twins' extremely close bond, what psychologists call the closest of all human relationships, had nearly been broken when, shortly after college, Mike was in a harrowing motorcycle accident that left him in a coma. "For those six days Marty was torn apart," Joni said. "He prayed and prayed, asking God to take care of the brother he loved. When Mike recovered, the twins joked that while Mike 'slept,' Marty had handled all the pain."

For these rugged individualists, Alaska with its deep contrasts of stunning mountain peaks, white-water fjords and slow-moving glaciers had a magnetic hold. Anchorage, its largest city, with over 225,000 people, became the twins' base, but they were most at home in its isolated wilds. Each gained a reputation for his hunting and fishing successes and both were known for their adventurous spirit. Marty's fledgling career as a hunting guide earned him mention in the September 1993 issue of American Hunter after he had served as a game packer and cook for a hunt for mountain goats the previous fall.

Both men had received full college football scholarships to Olivet Nazarene University in Illinois, where their well-matched size and strength made them a formidable one-two punch at defensive tackle. After graduating in 1987 and heading to Alaska, they took extensive training in mountain survival, a class taught, ironically, by an experienced mountaineer whose own attempt at climbing McKinley a day ahead of the Phelps threesome failed because he had developed "mountain illness." They also studied rappelling, snow-shelter building and outdoor medicine from well-known specialists, finding the classes fun, more recreational than serious academic pursuits.

If either twin wanted to know something, he always found a way to get an answer. For example, Marty learned many of his building skills by starting at the bottom, first carrying lumber for a builder and from there picking up what the contractor knew through direct experience. He understood that ability without training is like a sleeping bag without an inner filling, empty and useless.

For all their interest in rugged outdoor pursuits such as football, big-game hunting and now, for the first time mountain climbing, the twins had been raised by Joni Phelps and her husband, Stan, to be caring, God-fearing men. They loved each other, and they loved their mother, whose safety was the most important aspect of the climb. They strived to ensure it through care, concentration and the roped security of two separate harnesses, both of which were attached to each of them. One harness went around Joni's chest and the other around her legs and waist. The 50-foot rope passed from Mike through Joni's harnesses with their attached carabiners, strong metal clamps with locked releases, and then to Marty.

All three were prepared to control a fall through a metal attachment which allowed a restrained slide down a rope, a technique referred to by mountain climbers as "self-belay." Prior to slipping almost her full 5-feet 4-inch height into the crevasse as they closed in on the summit, Joni Phelps had used her ice ax to self-arrest twice as she slipped into fissures in the mountain's icy slopes. It had become the automatic thing to do. With the extra safety gear in the enormous packs her sons carried, she had felt confident in the success of the contest against nature, although none of the three had ever before attempted such a perilous adventure, or for that matter, ever climbed to the summit of a major peak.

The challenge they faced was considerable. According to the National Park Service rangers at Mt. McKinley, two-thirds of even the sighted climbers fail in their attempts to reach the ice-covered, 20,320-foot summit. Most are between 25 and 35 years of age, and only about one-quarter of them are women.

So the three dejected climbers were not alone in their sense of failure as they carefully edged back down the narrow spine of one of McKinley's treacherous upper ridges. They had come prepared for failure as well as success, but none of the Phelpses was accustomed to defeat.

Even as they carefully retraced their steps past the bowl-like camping area at 17,200 feet elevation from which the final leg of climbs to McKinley's pinnacle are launched and on down to 16,400 feet, an altitude in which

Joni's body could recuperate, the desire to go forward instead of back taunted them. Then, a providential meeting with a McKinley ranger who happened to be climbing in the opposite direction gave the climbers a glint of hope and rekindled Joni's ambition to reach the apex of North America's highest mountain.

"You've covered the worst section of the whole mountain," the experienced mountaineer encouraged them, "the most difficult terrain."

"Our spirits lifted a little," Joni would recall later, her short, wavy hair brushed away from her face, revealing the determined set of her chin and a unique glow in her eyes, "(We thought) maybe we could still make it if we returned to camp and recouped."

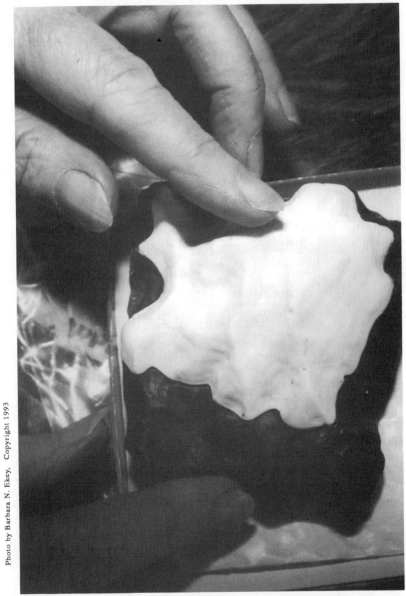

A chocolate map of Mt. McKinley

Chapter 2

"Faith, Hope, Love, these three -- but the greatest of these is love........."

A CHANCE TO DO MY BEST

"Southwest corner, climb up, right-hand turn, southeast, then a fish hook, climb to northwest area and swing around again," Joni Phelps recited as her fingertips deftly imprinted the West Buttress route of climbing Mt. McKinley in her mind.

As she closed her soft-blue eyes, her long, slender finger traced the route of the most dangerous steps of her life on a 4-by-4-inch chocolate image of the mountain, a gift from sons, Mike and Marty.

When Joni received the candy "map" on Christmas morning 1991, her eyes had filled with tears as the gift stirred recollections of her childhood dreams of climbing a mountain. "Thank you," she said tenderly, dispensing big twin hugs for a present that would come to symbolize a major change of all three of their lives.

"Let's climb the mountain!" the gray-haired, physically fit mother of four said, breaking into a wide, capricious smile. So excited that the words seemed to tumble out of her mouth, she assured, "I know we can do it!"

After 31 years of marriage, Stan Phelps was not surprised by his wife's proposal. He had seen her scuba diving, cycling, ice skating, even shooting a gun. He gave the seemingly impossible project his OK and, truth be told, may even have felt somewhat responsible for his wife's wanderlust. After all, he had stimulated her fascination with Alaska through tales of his hunting trips with the twins in the four years since the inseparable twosome had moved from the family's Warren, Pennsylvania hometown to make that last American frontier their home.

What a contrast the small provincial town of

Warren made with bustling Anchorage. With a population of around 14,000 in Warren itself and about 30,000 more in the surrounding area, the town was insulated from the outside world in many ways. Most of the Phelpses' neighbors would never consider heading to Alaska. Climbing a mountain, especially Mt. McKinley, would be as absurd as thoughts of going over Niagara Falls in a barrel.

But Stan and Joni Phelps' asphalt-shingled home, sited on a small, tree-screened lot, had been the embarking point for many individual and family adventures. There, protected from the dirt and constant noise of big oil rigs barreling down the street to the local refinery, they laid plans for and celebrated the successes of excursions far and near.

Just as it had been for the generations before them, the surrounding hills of Warren County afforded the family a handy "playground" for hunting white-tailed deer, black bear and rattlesnakes. An abundance of trout, walleye and muskie in the pure waters of the Allegheny River provided many evening meals.

Though cherished, these local experiences were mere appetizers for a family that hungered for greater adventure. Their economic means were modest, but the Phelpses were achievers whose lives were rich in a broader sense. The Christmas gift exchange took place in their home's 10-by-12-foot trophy room, transformed from a dining room to accommodate football trophies from the boys' high school and college days of championship play. A fully curled ram's horn, a 62-inch expanse of moose antlers and a bear's head also displayed there trumpeted success in additional outdoor pursuits. Permeating the rustic atmosphere of the room was a feeling that if Joni wanted to climb a mountain, she could climb a mountain, and her twin sons eagerly shouldered responsibility for making their mother's cherished dream a reality.

The following summer when Marty and Mike

again visited their family home, they and Joni sat down to seriously plan the adventure she had spontaneously proposed. From the onset, the climb had one golden rule: the bond that if anyone wasn't able to make it all the way, that they'd all go back down together.

"In the event that one would meet with death due to unpredictable circumstances, like an avalanche, we were to leave them there, resting with God, knowing that their soul was in heaven," Joni later told one of the many reporters who sought to chronicle their adventure. A strong spiritual philosophy had always guided the family to live life to the fullest constantly prepared to meet their maker.

After making their pact seated around the kitchen table, they prayed together for guidance.

CHILDHOOD YEARS

At the end of the same decade in which Amelia Earhart piloted a single-engine Lockheed Vega monoplane over the Atlantic to establish herself as the first woman to make the flight solo, the sixth of Henry and Rosella Sorensen's eight children was born and christened Joan. Growing up in a log cabin in the remote hills of the Allegheny National Forest prepared young Joni for a life of adventure and independence. She emulated Earhart from an early age and dreamed of someday establishing her own world record.

In the unadorned setting of the family's 35-acre homestead, she learned of nature and simple pleasures of rural life. Chickens and a cow helped feed the large Sorensen clan and on Sundays the family would go to the home of their Swedish grandmother on their mother's side, "Grandma Nellie." Before the family enjoyed one of the full-course dinners, grace was said, "God is great, God is good, Thank you for our food. Amen." Blackberry upside-down cake for dessert was the finishing touch to satisfying the hungry troop. Leftovers from the meal fed the Sorensens into the next week.

Grandma Nellie, who had immigrated to the United States as a teen, even baby-sat the brood while her mother worked outside the home for a few years to make ends meet.

Except for those few years of outside work, Rosella tended to children, home and garden. Henry Sorensen, a strong-minded Dane, worked as a machinist for a steel fabricating company. The whole family worshipped together, saying prayers before meals and upon retiring. Sundays were reserved for serving the Lord, and no business or physical labor beyond what was vitally necessary could be done.

From Monday through Saturday, however, hard work was what was expected of each family member. Joni learned to cook, clean and sew by helping her mother. There wasn't much money, even in the 1940s when most of the country was flourishing in the post-war boom. In later years Joni would become fond of saying, "We learned to make do with what we had."

Existing without luxuries or outside distractions gave her a feel for life and its importance at an early age. She loved to smell a flower or hear the beautiful song of a thrush. Nature in all its fullness brought her joy. The forest and hills became the Sorensen children's base for entertainment; climbing around a nearby slate quarry, riding old bikes and camping outside in a pup tent. They skated on a creek in the winter and dammed its waters to create a swimming hole in the summer.

Though just average in height having been full-grown at 5 feet, 4 inches at age 16, Joni was naturally coordinated. She would have loved dearly to have been on the girls basketball team at her high school, but the family couldn't provide transportation for the 10-mile trip into Warren for the games and practices. In high school Joni Sorensen, with her curly brown hair and sparkling blue eyes, seemed quiet to those that met her. She'd flash a friendly smile and a polite hello, but mostly she kept to herself.

She developed a special closeness to God during her teen-age years through the Nazarene Church, coming to believe fervently that life after death would be a joy if one lived in Christian piety. This strong religious upbringing served as the cornerstone of her adventurous life.

Much of Joni's free time was devoted to church activities of Sunday school, singing and evening prayer meetings. These put her in touch with an inner strength stemming from her discovery of the Lord and taught her to live according to the doctrines of her church and trust in God's love.

Developing from this seed of spirituality was her extraordinary power of will. It enabled her to overcome disappointment, economic difficulties and what to most people would seem as her insurmountable barrier, blindness. It was in these formative years that Joni learned that she was in the initial stages of the same inherited eye disease, retinitis pigmentosa, that had already afflicted her older sister.

Until then, and even after thanks to her faith, she viewed life as being a beautiful, winding path surrounded by gorgeous flowers and lined with trees in which the nightingale sings. She paused at every curve to smell the lush fragrance emanating from the blooms, to listen to nature's music and look over the Allegheny hills. Her positive nature eliminated the harsh realities of life, refused to acknowledge anything that was ugly or base or otherwise failed to meet her idealized frame of reference.

Joni loved school, though she couldn't always see the blackboard and also had trouble choosing skirts and blouses that matched each morning as she dressed. Her visual difficulties worsened in dim lighting, and many times she missed seeing objects lying on the floor. She didn't think much about those earliest signs of approaching blindness, however, and refused to even consider totally losing her sight.

Specially inspiring times for Joni were the hours

spent at the Nazarene Church's evening services with other teens. Her path was set when she went to the altar and gave her heart to the Lord. Once she made that surrender, she firmly believed, that was that.

Joyce McNaughton, her choir and youth director, became her guiding light. Joni needed the inspiration of an adult younger than her parents who encompassed the ideals she so fervently felt. On Thursday nights after choir practice, the group of teens and their director would head to Teaberry, a fellowship camp overlooking the picturesque hills of the Allegheny Forest, where they'd sing and discuss their beliefs around a campfire. On at least one weekend a month, McNaughton would invite Joni to spend the night with her and her family in their home. Sometimes their conversations, discussions of life and death, faith and healing, would last well into the night.

With stunning prescience, the 1957 Warren High School yearbook referred to graduating senior Joni

Sorensen as a "steady climber" and described her as studious and serious. After taking a year off to work for the telephone company, Bell of Pennsylvania, she enrolled at Eastern Nazarene College, where the ever-adventuresome young woman rounded out the typical freshman curriculum with a course in rappelling. "I liked the freedom it gave me," said Joni several years later of risking life and limb while leaping spider-like from rock to rock on a single rope tether. "It was fun."

While at college she embraced fully the new experiences, but academic subjects were a challenge to her failing eyesight. She put extra emphasis on her reading, fully believing that not only would this concentration improve her grades, but that it might in fact strengthen her eyes. She hadn't yet developed the keen memory skills which would later inform her perceptions of the McKinley climb.

When Joni returned home in the spring, her mother took her to nearby Jamestown, New York to have her eyes examined by a specialist. The diagnosis was issued as a blunt and shattering blow. "You've damaged your eyes with all that reading," the doctor said. "You are going blind."

Hard-working Rosella Sorensen was furious with the doctor. Why couldn't he have given her daughter just a thread of hope? Why did he have to be so harsh and destroy her dreams.

But despair at being torn away from the liberating promise of academic life simply led Joni to tap the inner strength of her close relationship with God. She became determined that faith, not blindness, would control her life.

One bright point during this trying period was becoming better acquainted with Stan Phelps, the friend of a classmate she had dated at Warren High School. The muscular, 5-foot, 10-inch Phelps, who had pitched a blazing fastball while serving in the U.S. Navy, stimulated her love of nature and physical challenges and more importantly accepted her impending blindness. Together they rode his motorcycle through the unspoiled beauty of the Allegheny National Forest and reveled in the excitement of their escapades. In 1960 the couple wed, forging a partnership of mutual support and encouragement in the pursuit of the rigorous adventures they both relished.

Joni and Stan continued their pursuit of nature, often venturing out on the same motorcycle that carried them through yearlong courtship and on to their honeymoon camping excursion. On one memorable occasion, they had stopped to appreciate the forest scenery when an enormous black bear suddenly appeared nearby. Fearing for their lives, the couple instantly climbed a tree, where they remained for several hours as the bear searched the ground below them. Meanwhile, back in Warren, their singing group waited for the usually punctual pair, wondering what had happened. Finally the adventurers came running into the church and excitedly recounted their experience.

But as her life progressed from childhood to adulthood and marriage afforded prospects of a growing family, Joni's visual world, as a consequence of the hereditary, degenerative condition retinitis pigmentosa, receded from light to dark.

A cure still has not been discovered for this disease which is caused when the retina, the light-sensitive inner coat of the eye on which light rays focus, develops splotches or strands of black pigment. Taking large doses of vitamin A has proven to postpone blindness in some cases and an opaque shell over one eye could possibly help preserve vision by excluding direct light from the retina, but most of its victims eventually go blind.

Joni's progressive blindness followed a typical pattern for RP. Beginning in her youth with her inability to see clearly in low light and to decipher colors, her vision gradually diminished by early adulthood until only a limited field remained. With proper lighting, she in early adulthood could see what was directly in front of her, but not the full panorama of the Pennsylvania countryside where the Phelpses made their home. Before long she no longer could distinguish faces, but could see an outline of a dark image against a light-colored wall.

In her early thirties, Joni joined the family for what was to become her last family biking escapade. Using her own vision as her guide she relished this excursion along the beautiful forest roads by Jake's Rocks, a popular Warren County tourist attraction by the Allegheny Reservoir. She treasured recollections of that day with the wind blowing in her face, the smell of the forest and the freedom to explore God's creation.

Chapter 3

"To Love is to risk not being loved in return..."

DOUBLE INDEMNITY

"Twins!" At best, the word spawned trepidation in the hearts of most expectant parents of a generation ago. Over the medical hazards, the economic strains and physical demands kept most parents, especially the mother, bleary-eyed and perpetually catatonic. Most Warren residents, though fascinated with the mysticism of double births, believed they were a mistake of nature, a burden to bear.

But Joni and Stan were thrilled in December 1963 to welcome home their healthy twin sons, feeling doubly blessed. The doctor said Mike and Marty were not identical since they had developed in two different uterine sacks. But Mike, who was first born, and Marty, who followed a few minutes later, looked exactly alike and both weighed about 6 pounds. When the chunky twins smiled broadly, looking so nearly identical, even their proud and protective father could not be sure which was which.

Jubilant as she was at this double blessing, Joni's work was extra trying; twofold diapers, twice the midnight feedings, and stereo crankiness at teething time. She already had an energetic daughter who hadn't yet turned 2. She knew in her heart that she had been given this extra challenge for a reason, however, and prayed to God for strength and direction.

Even while still in the hospital, she concentrated on sleeping whenever she could, knowing that she would need added stamina for the twin challenge. Checking on her before she went home, her doctor asked, "Have you been able to get some sleep?"

"Yes, whenever possible."

The physician smiled and responded, "Good! You're going to do just fine."

Pen & Pencil Drawing by Joanne Oviatt

The Phelps Twins

41

Returning home with the demands of cooking, cleaning and caring for her infant sons and daughter Judy kept Joni extremely busy. Each night the young family clustered together in prayer: "Now I lay me down to sleep I pray the Lord my soul to keep..." The quiet of the night which followed was many times interrupted by double cries.

Joni had two advantages; Stan worked nights so he could help her during the day, and she learned to sleep whenever the twins napped at the same time. Almost 30 years later she recalled this experience with a smile and said, "I knew I'd be able to control my body on the climb because I learned to do it starting with the twins."

Family Unity

Joni's advancing visual problem brought a close young family even closer, all championing the mother they loved. Shunting aside the inevitable depression and frustration of going blind, she developed through the special vision engendered by her faith and optimism, the ability to put trust in others. With this trust and love came the assurance that they would care for her. She, in return, would do her utmost to take care of them.

Humor pervaded the Phelps home, often centering on the twins, who early on displayed the curiosity and daring inherited from their parents. They loved exploring and rushed home to tell about their adventures, offering unique descriptions of discoveries they had made.

Once after returning home from kindergarten, the impish matched pair talked a mile a minute, trying to relate the same tale simultaneously. Their father, after struggling to hear both of them, finally said, "I can only listen to one of you at a time."

"But Dad," they instantly responded in unison, "you have two ears."

The couple didn't grow grass in their backyard, they'd tell people with obvious pride, because they had kids. In addition to the twins and Judy, the older daughter, the family eventually grew to include a younger son, Jim. To keep his rambunctious offspring occupied, Stan Phelps created a toy from a giant garage door spring, which the children used to zigzag wildly through the air. He also invented a cart for the nearby railroad tracks that used tire rims as wheels. It helped set a lifelong pattern in the Phelps children of venturing far afield and living life a bit dangerously.

"I don't know what I would have done without Stan," said Joni with emphasis. "He made everything possible. He was always encouraging the children and me to reach for our dreams."

Once the family nursed a motherless fawn named Scottie back to health before giving it to the Pennsylvania Game Commission for release. This experience, like many others, fostered a caring nature in the twins and their siblings. Friends relate stories of how Marty in particular would make the most rejected person his friend. "He didn't see that they were fat or different, just that they had value," observed Mike Phelps of his brother.

In high school Mike and Marty played tackle and guard on the Warren Dragons' football team. "Many times their coach would get them mixed up during practice, especially when they'd done something wrong," recalled their father. "Neither would say anything and afterward the whole family would laugh about the wrong one getting chewed out."

Joni and Stan never missed a game even in the harshest of weather. Through the aid of a radio and headset as well as the hush of the hikes and responses of the crowds, Joni followed each play down the field and "saw" in her mind the ball being moved back and forth. She cheered loudly for her sons and their team when a touchdown was scored.

Mike's position as a guard on the football team carried over into the twins' antics off the gridiron, such as the time he stood watch as Marty, the healer, sewed up a friend's arm in the bathroom of their home. The boys had been playing and somehow their chum got cut in the arm by Marty's knife.

"Mart, I'm not going to the hospital," his friend said. "You'll have to do it yourself."

When Marty returned with needle and thread, his friend added, "Sterilize it." Marty dutifully got out a pack of matches and blackened the needle, made his stitches and then applied a Band-Aid to hide the evidence. "He did a good job," he said later with a chuckle. "I'll carry the scar with me forever."

Like the shadowy raven of Alaska, known in mythology and in reality for constantly being a trickster, Mike and Marty used their matching darks looks, similar handwriting and common physical skills to play games and glean an advantage when needed. The duplicity of being twins often doubled Mike and Marty's fun in high school. For example, when Mike needed to go take his driver's license, Marty, who had a free period, sat through a class in Mike's seat with no one the wiser.

When at Olivet College, the brothers had different roommates, but they were still always together. After a successful hunt, the rough-and-ready duo would flaunt convention and tan hides in their dorm rooms, displaying for all their friends the pungent trophies.

What also became obvious to their friends at the Christian school was their strong faith. Mike and Marty prayed together on a daily basis and shared their beliefs with their many friends. But it fell on Marty to be the encourager who gave undeniable support, listening to troubles and consoling heartaches. He'd tell his friends, "You're doing good!" and urge a loser to think as a winner.

Well marked in Marty's Bible were these words of scripture: "Whether we live, we live unto the Lord, whether we die, we die unto the Lord. Therefore, whether we live or die, we are the Lord's." On the side in his pinched handwriting was the notation, "I want to be like Paul." He admired the Apostle's committed and passionate nature, making no compromise where his faith was concerned. Like Paul, too, Marty felt humbled by God's blessing and considered himself a debtor.

And, of course, it was Paul who was struck blind by God in a dramatic act of transformation. The impact of blindness was a force Marty knew well.

Chapter 4

"To Hope is to risk despair...."

A GLIMMER OF LIGHT

A silent subtext running through the family's beloved and well-worn accounts of the children's growing-up years was Joni Phelps' deteriorating vision. By age 35, when the twins were about 10, she was totally blind. Unlike her sisters, who lost their eyesight a few years later and resigned themselves to quiet activities, Joni remained vibrant and never shrank from a challenge. "When opportunity knocks, I'm there," she'd say. "Being blind is not an insurmountable challenge."

Anxious to keep her life free of boundaries, she obtained her first guide dog in 1974. The white German shepherd, Duffy, held her undeniable trust to lead the way, giving her independence of movement and freedom to meet new opportunities.

With Duffy in tow, the family traveled to New

York City that summer, and Joni Phelps' very last visual memory is the Statue of Liberty, its monumental, 152-foot silhouette steadfast against the sky as daughter Judy read the inscription on the plaque at its base:

"Not like the brazen giant of Greek fame, with conquering limbs astride from land to land: Here at our sea-washed, sunset gates shall stand a mighty woman with a torch, whose flame is the imprisoned lightning, and her name Mother of exiles....." Judy read as the foreign languages of other visitors babbled in the background. "Keep, ancient lands, your storied pomps! cries she with silent lips. Give me your tired, your poor, your huddled masses yearning to breathe free....I lift my lamp beside the golden door!"

The memory lingered, permanently implanted on Joni's mind. Years after she would still close her eyes with reverence and concentration whenever speaking of the symbolic moment.

When her eyes became permanently dark except

for dim awareness of very bright light, she leaned heavily on such memories, on the guidance of her family and of course on her guide dog. Duffy not only served as her guide physically, but helped lead the whole family into acceptance of her blindness. Setting the pattern that one day would be followed by Mike and Marty on Mt. McKinley, the children shared the dog's work, learning to excel at describing what their mother's failing eyes could no longer define.

Joni continued to cook and clean just as before, except everyone had to remember to push in chairs around the old oak kitchen table and close cupboard doors so she didn't walk into them. Stan continued to work his night job and helped to look after the children during the day, constantly giving them new challenges and encouraging them to triumph.

"My eyes changed so gradually that it's hard to say when the different stages occurred, but since my mid-30s I've been considered totally blind," Joni has said, immediately defying any pitying thoughts by adding, "I love a chance to do my best."

Just like Phelpses' backyard, she never let any grass grow under her feet. She desired to let everyone know that her world isn't dark, but filled with beauty. That she had not been a blind individual, but a specially blessed woman who just happened not to see in the usual fashion. Her flower gardens remained filled with fragrant blossoms and colorful blooms as always, but with one exception: after she became blind, her visions of the plot never were marred by weeds.

She continued to display her creativity through quilting, but needed to follow the straight pins set to hold the seams by her first born, her beautiful brown-haired, brown-eyed daughter Judy. Joni weeded the garden in much the same way, relying on God, she said, to guide her fingers to the weeds and not the flowers as she amazed her neighbors with her gardening skills. "It was hard to believe she couldn't see." commented one friend who lived nearby. "She did a better and faster job of weeding without her eyes than I could do being able to see."

"When the children were out of the house, I decided it was my time to do things," she explained in her firm, but enthusiastic way. "I knew I didn't want to weigh 150 pounds when I was 50, and that sitting around the house was boring."

About a year before she reached that half-century milestone, Joni joined the Calvary Singers, a group of Christian women who had been meeting for over 20 years. She relished the spirit of the group, their discussions of scripture and prayer. Through this group she rediscovered her enjoyment of social activities and the support of this concerned, intimate group of women with whom she instantly had rapport. Singing had always brought her joy, and true to scripture, making a joyful noise lifted her closer to heaven.

Accompanied by her guide dog, (she had three in

succession, two Labrador retrievers following the shepherd named Duffy), Joni went out of her way to share her special insights with others, at times appearing at three different places in a day: first a kindergarten perhaps, then a nursing home and last the Warren State Hospital, a facility for those with emotional difficulties. Her only regret was that she couldn't speak at all the places that asked her. But, with practicing and performing with her singing friends, she had to set limits.

Her inspiration upon the sick and disabled was evident when she spoke in April 1993 of her blindness. During a break in the Calvary Singers' performance, she talked about being blind and how her current guide dog, Shear Pleasure, assisted her. After her short presentation, the group of 30 elderly sat up noticeably straighter and joined the singers unfalteringly in a song. A nurse remarked that one lady who hadn't uttered a word in six years started to talk.

An unspoken realization seemed to have overcome

them, that all are handicapped in some way, and none is without obstacles in his or her life. What's important is having the courage to overcome them.

Cross-country Skiing

Chapter Five

"To place your ideas and dreams before the crowd is to risk loss..."

CAN I TRY IT?

Joni Phelps had never been one to be left out of any adventure. Whether it was climbing the Allegheny hills or kayaking, scuba diving or cross-country skiing miles from home, she participated, focusing on learning every detail of how to safely accomplish her goal.

"Can I try it?" were words which family and friends knew well. She wanted to do it all, never letting her lack of sight get in the way. She had a knack for making those who heard of her adventures think that if Joni could climb a mountain, they could conquer the "foothills" in their own lives.

Personal achievements seemed a natural for this woman, who raised her four children to believe that everything is possible for those who use their minds, trained bodies and determination; calculated risks, she believed, are worth taking.

What brought the keen will to achieve sharply into focus was meeting Richard Casey, a New York City lawyer who talked at a guide dog training school about Ski for Light, an international group which coordinates sporting events for the visually impaired. Its motto, "If I can do this, I can do anything," dovetailed neatly with Joni's own positive approach. Immediately excited by the prospects of not only skiing, but experiencing the thrill of competing, she just wanted to know where she could sign up.

Ski for Light is a unique sports program which enables blind individuals an opportunity to experience outdoor activities such as cross-country skiing in the winter, and bicycling, rock climbing and golfing in the summer. Through the use of sighted guides, the athlete trains the mind to receive the given directions and then control the body's response. Competition is encouraged at a level at which they can achieve success.

This organization cultivated others to embrace the determination Joni had achieved on her own; to never surrender to blindness. Instead of focusing on what she couldn't do, she enthusiastically tried new sports, relishing the fun of it all. Her nickname among her friends from Ski for Light became "Slow down, Joni." She seemed to be racing to put her name in the record books, joining the ranks of other famous women athletes she had heard about: runner Wilma Rudolph, who won the Sullivan Award as the nation's outstanding amateur athlete; three-time world record holder Babe Dedrikson Zaharias, who shined in track and field; and speed skater/cyclist Sheela Young, who became a world champion in 1973. Even Joni's family album touted a second cousin, Ray Sorensen, who also grew up in Warren and competed in the 1948 Olympics in London, England, as part of the U.S. gymnastics team.

Intrigued by rifle shooting, Joni soon discovered

she could hit a bullseye as effectively as the rest of her family, only her technique was different. Through the use of an electronic sighting system, she created her own "crosshairs" by moving her gun first vertically and then horizontally. As she listened to the audio signals, she made adjustments until the tones were as low as possible, indicating she was in line. Through a camp for the blind in the small town of Sherman in northeastern Pennsylvania, Joni not only learned this shooting technique but also won awards for her skill in baseball and golf.

Her son-in-law Jack Browne related a typical episode, one in which he learned that his mother-in-law was never to be left out. During a weekend Frisbee shoot in the late 1980s where one family member would toss the plastic saucer into the air and another would try to hit the moving target, Joni piped up that she wanted to try. Without speaking, the Phelps clan threw a number of Frisbees and yelled for Joni to shoot, except this time it was without benefit of the audio sighting device. When the sound of a bullet hitting the target suggested her shot had landed, the Frisbee throwers all applauded. Not until long after did Joni learn that she hadn't hit her target, but a backpack lying on the ground.

In 1989 she learned to cross-country ski with a guide beside her giving her directions, and by 1990 her innate competitive spirit had propelled her into national skiing contests. In her competitors she found allies. "These new friends I made were so exciting, an inspiration to me because many of them were professionals, succeeding in the world of business," she would tell friends back home, respect resonating in her voice.

SECOND IN THE WORLD

Joni was 50 when she started competing in cross-country competitions sponsored by Ski for Light. She vividly remembered her first formal ski race in 1990 at

Bozman, Montana. As her name and number were called out over the paging system, she was cheered on to the finish line by a large crowd. She had put every ounce of energy into the race, thinking along the way of Mike and Marty's physical challenges in high school. By chance, she'd been given number 74, the number of Marty's football jersey.

"You share in those feelings of challenge and competition," she later said with a smile, remembering attending every one of the boys' football games, rooting on the action she could not see, but which seemed to charge the very air with electricity.

"I had the feeling that the twins were rooting for me. I knew that they never quit in football. Then it came to the end and this number is ringing in my ears. It was like a confirmation that they were with me in spirit crossing the finish line."

Joni felt euphoric as the ribboned medallion was draped around her neck, and tears flowed from her eyes.

In 1992 she flew to Beitostolen, Norway, where 1,000 skiers had come from 18 different countries to compete in the Ski for Light Olympics, called Ridderanen by the Norwegians. Her heart raced before the competition, and when the national anthem was sung, a respectful silence underlined the sense of anticipation. As she walked away from the ceremony, a German patted her shoulder and then grabbed her arm, saying in rough, guttural English, "Strong woman," as if to say she could surmount whatever obstacle she desired, even a mountain. Clearly others recognized her strength.

She earned accolades for her accomplishments in Norway, winning two second-place medals in her age bracket: one in a 20-kilometer competition and the other in the biathlon, in which cross-country skiers make four stops to shoot at targets set up along a 12.5-mile course. All that stood between her and the gold was an equally determined Norwegian woman named Doreen Hardwick, a year or two her senior.

Gratifying though her fine showing in international competition was, Joni Phelps had another, greater achievement in mind during that trip. This was the goal she had hatched on a whim a few months before as her family gathered in their rustic trophy room, exchanging Christmas gifts.

Though deeply personal, her dream of climbing Mt. McKinley was no secret to her close friends. When in Minnesota for the March 1993 Ski for Light competition, John Claricoat, a lawyer who flew from London for the event, commented on the dangers of Joni's plan when he quipped, "We'll have a memorial service for Joni before she leaves."

She laughed at his dark humor but understood the serious feelings behind the words. She knew what lay ahead.

Always a physically active woman, Joni, with husband Stan as her guide, regularly hiked, biked and skied with her friends from the Allegheny Outdoor Club, a group of vigorous nature lovers in her native Warren County. The climbing of Mount McKinley, however, required the investment of an extra 40 hours per week of training for both mind and body, beginning in the fall of 1992.

Each day Stan returned from his supply room work at Bell of Pennsylvania ready to help his wife prepare her most vital piece of equipment, her own body for the ultimate challenge. Together they loaded her pack, snowshoes, crampons and collapsible ski pole into their well-worn 1980 Chevrolet Malibu. The black Labrador Shear Pleasure would seat himself on his master's lap, wagging his tail so hard it knocked the lint off her parka.

Driving down the final section of a one-lane dirt road which most drivers in four-wheel drive vehicles would not attempt, Stan maneuvered the bouncing old car around large holes, patches of ice and sharp turns. After arriving at a favored spot in the hills of Allegheny National Forest, Joni donned heavy outerwear, boots, harnesses and ropes.   Topping all, as might be expected of a mother who loved to bake, she prepared for the most dangerous steps in her life by climbing the undulating hills carrying a special 50-pound cargo in her backpack: 10 five-pound sacks of flour or sugar.

Throughout the winter's snow and ice and well into the spring, Joni hiked 2-3 miles straight up these rough hills, taking slow and measured steps as she went. Along the way she built not only stamina, but the intense concentration needed to climb Mt. McKinley.

When twin Mike and younger son Jim, an emergency-room nurse in Charlotte, N.C., visited in early May 1993, Joni practiced obeying Mike's commands. "Drop and dig in," he shouted in his strong baritone voice. Instantly she would fall straight to the ground, rehearsing the life-saving technique intended to stop potentially fatal slips and falls. Rocks, which by then were free of their winter cushion of snow, would sometimes dig into her body just as her ice ax dug into the ground. Still, she obeyed, never complaining.

In another activity which prepared her mentally as well as physically, Joni slept outside on the porch of her northwestern Pennsylvania home through the long, cold winter, familiarizing her body with hard surfaces and sub-zero nights. She'd crawl into her dark blue sleeping bag wearing the same "snuggies," polypropylene tops and bottoms with a "back hatch" similar to one-piece long underwear in which she would live throughout the 18-day climb of McKinley.

Sons Mike and Marty spent over $2,000 making sure their mother had the best mountain survival clothing, the top of the line in everything. Joni practiced putting on her vapor-barrier bunny boots, snug-fitting caps and the jackets she would be wearing during the climb. Her layers of polypropylene would prevent the famous McKinley winds from reaching her body, insulating her from temperatures as low as minus 40 degrees Fahrenheit.

Weather permitting, Joni walked three days a week

to the YMCA for a regimen of aerobic and Nautilus exercises. When she strapped Shear Pleasure into his harness for the mile hike, the dog's usual playful nature changed to all business. During the trip down the main highway, he led Joni safely by the passing cars and across intersections. After a strenuous workout which included repeatedly bench pressing 35 pounds, exercises promoting trunk flexibility, timed sit-ups, and 10 miles registered on the Nordik track, she satisfied her sweet tooth and need for socializing by heading with a friend to a local cafe for decaffeinated coffee and pastry.

Before Joni left home and headed to Alaska on Mother's Day 1993, Linda Taylor, YMCA personal fitness program director, tested the success of her six-month regimen. The profile of body composition, cardiovascular fitness, strength and endurance showed her to be at the top fitness ranking for women her age. When compared to women of all ages, her muscular strength and endurance equaled the excellence of a 20-year-old and put her at 90 percentile.   Even in the midst of the climb, her blood oxygen levels would measure in the high 80s, a desired level of top athletes, prompting the McKinley ranger who did the test to exclaim, "Lady, you must be a horse."

All the while, to satisfy her own need to know the terrain she would be traveling, she studied her two three-dimensional maps, the small chocolate one from her sons and a large relief map of rugged Alaskan landscape.   The 20,320 feet elevation at Mt. McKinley's summit would make a total distance of 19 miles of climbing interspersed by stops every short distance.

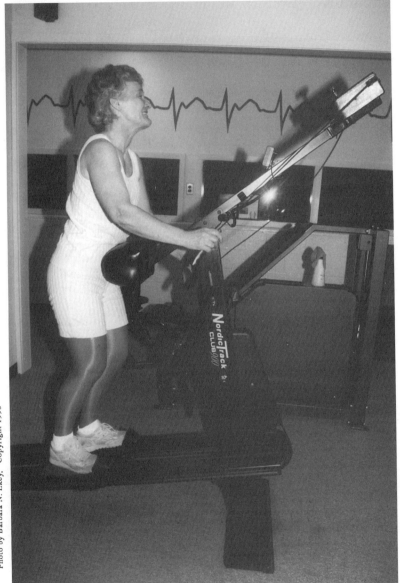

Rigorous Training

Chapter Six

"To try is to risk failure..."

GLACIAL ADVANCES

Without fanfare, Joni boarded a plane at the Erie airport on Mother's Day. Emotion knotted in her throat as she kissed her husband and hugged her dog, who would be left behind, temporarily replaced as Joni's guide by her sons. Escorted by a flight attendant, she slowly progressed down the walkway to the plane's door for the first leg of her journey.

She rode a crowded commercial airliner, but her transcontinental journey had more in common with that pioneering solo crossing of North America made in 1932 by Amelia Earhart than with her fellow modern-day travelers. If Joni's trip was a success, she would have her long-dreamed-of place in the pantheon of women adventurers. If it was not...

Only one blind person had reached international

acclaim for mountain climbing, albeit but on a mountain considered one-tenth as difficult as Mount McKinley, a walk-up in comparison. In 1880, after climbing France's Mont Blanc ("white mountain"), which rises to 15,771 feet elevation in France near its borders with Switzerland and Italy, Francis Joseph Campbell, a middle-aged educator of the blind who lost his eyesight at age 3, became a Fellow of the Royal Geographical Society. In 1909 he was knighted by King Edward VII in recognition of his pioneering of a new tact in learning without physically seeing.

The risk Joni was taking in each step toward Mt. McKinley's summit called to mind a poem (author unknown) which she used to read when speaking to students and adults. The verse reflected her feelings exactly; "To laugh is to risk being a fool, To weep is to risk being sentimental, To reach out to another is to risk involvement, To express ones feelings is to risk expressing your true self, To place your ideas and dreams before the crowd is to risk loss, To love is to risk not being loved in return, To live is to risk dying, To hope is to risk despair, To try it all is to risk failure..." Above all else, one must take risks in order to live a full life.

Upon the jet's early evening arrival at Anchorage International Airport, the pilot showed her to the baggage area where Marty, after snapping a few photos, greeted his mother with open arms. Since Mike had to work in order to save his days off for the climb, Marty and the twin's black lab, who waited in the car and welcomed Joni with excited licks, comprised the full welcoming committee.

Family friends grilled venison and bear meat on an open pit barbecue that evening and laughed about the hearty appetites of the twins, especially Marty's love of eating. The next morning Joni explored a little of Anchorage with Marty as he took care of last-minute shopping and guided her discovery of local color. When they encountered a gigantic moose standing at the roadside, he commented, "He's so big we could drive under him."

During a taxidermy shop visit, Joni felt the claws of an 11-foot bear similar to the one the boys had bagged in Alaska the summer before. A stuffed wolf stood in the corner, reminding hunters of their abundance in the wilds of Alaska. Only on Mt. McKinley were these hardy predators unable to survive, and even adventurous, high-flying ravens are rarely seen on this stark mountain.

At the U.S. Post Office, Marty requested the special Alaska stamps depicting an old pickup truck on the road to Mt. McKinley as a special memento of their adventure. Wherever they went, people spoke highly of the twins, reaffirming their mother's already absolute confidence in their skill. Still, in the unfamiliar surroundings, she was beginning to have misgivings about her own abilities. The subtle doubts that began to unsettle her remained unspoken and even in retrospect would only be surmised through subtle hints. As if to test her, fate tossed in a delay.

When Mike and Marty registered their climb with park rangers in Talkeetna, they learned that because of a horrendous snow storm, there would be a two-day delay before they could take the short airplane hop to the Kahiltna Glacier.

Finally on Friday, May 14, a bright red Cesna plane flew them to the 7,000-foot elevation base camp, again without fanfare. Greeting them at this gathering point from a rustic quonset hut was Ann Marie Duquette, an attractive blond of about 30 years, whom Joni called "Friendly Annie." She helped them with their gear and would serve as their communications liaison while on the mountain, passing along weather reports each night on the radio.

More than 1,000 climbers from over 20 countries climb Mt. McKinley each year with the majority using the popular West Buttress route, the same one the Phelps party chose. Encircled by lofty peaks of the Alaskan

Mountain Range, the base camp was dotted with tents of other waiting teams. The Phelpses soon learned that there would be an additional unplanned interlude on this level base area on the southeast section of the glacier, but that they would be given overnight accommodations in a ranger's cabin. Unlike the worrisome holdup in Anchorage, this extra day's break proved a godsend. Joni had time to make her first adjustment to the altitude and thin mountain air. Eager as she was to begin their assault, she wanted to avoid even the initial signs of altitude sickness; the loss of appetite, headache and shortness of breath that was a consequence of climbing too fast.

THE GREAT ONE

Even by sighted standards, climbing McKinley is considered extremely dangerous. The summit of Denali, or "Great One," which was first reached on June 7, 1913, by American missionary and explorer Hudson Stuck, proves unobtainable to two-thirds of those who try. Most fail because they neglect to secure themselves with ropes or are ill-prepared physically for the climb. Others succumb to the unpredictable dangers of the ever-changing mountain. A McKinley park ranger talked about a horrible disaster in the summer of 1967 when all seven men in a climbing expedition were literally blown off the mountain. By the time the Phelps trio started their climb of the mountain, these deaths had to be erased from their thoughts.

Their focus had to be solely on their climb, the one-foot-in-before-the-other, pick-and-crampon act of ascending the imposing face of McKinley. To do that, they wanted to proceed by themselves, without interference; no press and no photographers allowed. They didn't want anyone stopping them just because Joni was blind, so they strived to keep it a secret.

On Saturday, May 15, another small, tightly packed plane dropped Mike, Marty and Joni Phelps off at the glacial landing strip. Only a small portion of their

500 pounds of gear and food could be carried on the flight, and so a second trip had to be made with the extra gear, which was just dumped from the low-flying plane as it buzzed the trio.

The climbers immediately buried a cache of their extras and checked their three lightweight citizens band radios which each carried for communication among themselves and also with the ranger stations. Extra batteries were carried inside their jackets to keep them warm, assuring backup power.

Slathering sun screen on the scant exposed areas of their skin, they set out immediately and unceremoniously, groping their way along. "It was so hard at first," Joni later said with emphasis. "We hadn't had time to practice, so we had to work it all out as we went along."

Just keeping her body centered over her boots and taking short breaths of the thin mountain air posed a problem. When the surface would drop down or rise up, Joni had a difficult time determining where she was placing her foot, many times overcompensating.

In the beginning, as they moved along the relatively flat upper surface of the glacier punctuated by unseen crevasses and chasms in the ice hidden beneath a covering of snow, Joni concentrated on putting one foot in front of the other and keeping her balance. Testing and feeling the packed snow for soft spots and holes with her two collapsible poles, she would many times be in the lead, followed by Marty and then Mike, as the trio inched along.

They learned to communicate in a verbal shorthand that conserved their breath as they created strategies for the climb. Sometimes Joni would misread the command, but most of the time it proved to be a twin who erred; a "step up" was ordered when a "step down" was meant, and miscues for right and left most often tripped them up.

As they ascended, Marty's clipped descriptions of the weathered faces of the people traveling down from the summit alerted Joni to the mountain's hazards. "Mom, their skin is dry and scaly. They look haggard," Marty would report. She made a mental note to use the extra-rich moisturizer she had brought.

Mike and Marty, carrying a portion of their mother's gear in addition to their own, shouldered enormous packs filled with the safety equipment and provisions that would be vital to making a successful climb. At all times, a shovel for making an emergency snow shelter protruded from one of their packs. In addition, they each pulled a sled weighing over 100 pounds, encumbered with "spares" such as the extra ropes, ice screws and harnesses.

Getting into the rhythm with cautious steps across snow of varying depths proved difficult. As the first day's leg of the climb wore on, they were moving along steadily when Joni's foot suddenly disappeared from view, dropping into a hole. With Mike and Marty's rope preventing a further plunge, she edged her way back up to a standing position. "You left a blue foot print," the boys told their mother of the first test of the safety ropes, a foreshadowing of several others that followed.

They knew the risks inherent in climbing McKinley, but didn't talk about them, then or ever during the climb. What the tired but excited climbers would do that first night and every night for the rest of the climb was to say their prayers, asking God to guide them safely to the summit.

As much as anything, Joni found the initial climb psychologically difficult because she didn't know how it would turn out. As she plodded along, questions started to rise from her sub-conscious; "Is it foolish to risk our lives just to pursue a dream?" or "Am I really meant to do this?"

But her doubts seemed to fade somewhat because the trek from the starting point went down instead of up, instilling positive thought, "I think I can reach my goal." Two-mile-long Heartbreak Hill dropped down to 6,800 feet in elevation and this increased the oxygen levels in her lungs and put less stress on her body.

From there the terrain again edged upward, and at 7,800 feet they made their first camp. There the twins set out to create the first of many protective walls fashioned from light-weight blocks of hard-packed snow. The neat and effective shelter earned praise from other climbers. Their bright blue tent's flag -- the word "MOM" at the top and with "Mike" and "Marty" descending from the two "M's." -- waved in the wind, and to a tired but euphonic Joni, its sharp snapping signaled to all that she, in particular, was free to follow her dream.

Even through Joni was fatigued, sleeping was difficult because of the altitude. She kept waking up due to her need to concentrate on taking the short breaths required to get enough oxygen into her system.

Mike slept in the prime middle position with his brother and mother on either side. They had to put their clothing, extra caps and some gear inside their sleeping bags to keep them dry from the dampness of their condensing breath inside the tent.

Joni's culinary specialties, her dinner rolls from scratch and mouthwatering sweet rolls, were nowhere in sight on the climb. The trio carried meals for 25 days with them, 75 meals for each, 225 in all. Because of the physical limitations of setting up camp in subzero temperatures, their menus involved easy preparation, foods like instant rice, oatmeal, raisins and peanuts, and a daily vitamin supplement. Spartan as the diet was, pains were taken to ensure enough food was always at hand.

Three hours each morning were devoted to melting enough snow and ice in a bright red cooking can fired with a butane burner to make the 18 liters of water the trio required daily to prevent dehydration due to the dry air and moisture lost through breathing. Liquids also helped prevent frostbite, and each carried his or her own water bottle inside a insulated bag which Mike had designed for the climb. To make the melted snow palatable, they added fruit flavoring.

With the trek up Ski Hill on the second day, the team commenced to truly climb. Joni carefully followed the carved steps made by previous climbers, again using two ski poles to search the area immediately in front of her for firm footing.

The short-lived secret of Joni's blindness got out when another group of adventurers took special interest in the way in which the trio functioned. As the Phelpses headed for a place to make their second camp at 9,400 feet in a broad flat area which needed to be probed for crevasses, some Marines discussed Joni's unique climbing technique.

"What do you think is wrong with that woman?" one young man asked, loud enough for the Phelpses to hear.

"She's blind," a colleague responded.

"Oh, no, she can't be, she's leading the pack."

As the Phelps trio got closer and the Marines got a better look at Joni who wore wraparound goggles as she forged ahead, they heard the voices of the twins. One recruit exclaimed, "She is too blind. That fellow behind her is giving her directions."

Curiosity got the best of the Marine group as they asked Joni to confirm that she couldn't see. She said yes, and they were impressed that she and her sons were climbing together as a family team.

After the encounter, Joni became known among other adventurers on the busy route as "Mom of the Mountain."

Memorized Technique

Chapter Seven

"To reach out to another is to risk involvement..."

FAIL-SAFE FOCUS

At 11,000 feet in elevation, a series of small hills provided protection from the furious winds. The team took advantage of this shelter from the unrelenting gusts for their third night's camp. After again carefully probing two to three feet down in a circular area over a diameter of about 25 feet to check for hidden crevasses, they pitched their tent in a location that soon became crowded with shelters of other climbers..

While the twins visited their neighbors, Joni treasured her solitude, reflecting on the day's climb and anticipating the next. Suddenly the whirl of a helicopter overhead caused a pang of concern as Joni thought that someone had encountered a serious problem, but when the sons returned to the tent, Marty assured her, "The helicopter was just doing a practice run."

In actuality, the chopper was on no mere practice run. A 31-year-old U.S. Marine, who was close to death because of AMS, acute mountain sickness (a condition where the lungs filled with fluid,) had to be taken to the Anchorage Hospital in an effort to save his life. "The boys low-keyed the dangers to me, but I knew there was a problem," Joni said after the climb. "I could hear the concern in their voices and later discovered through climbing friends that it was a rescue."

What she learned was that the military enlistee had suffered a bout of the flu just before the climb, and had been fed intravenously to make him stronger. Again weakened by the time the group got past Windy Corner about 3 days' climb up the face of McKinley, the Marine collapsed. A ranger, interrupting a sergeant's yells of recrimination, examined the fallen man and instantly called for the helicopter to fly him to the hospital. A disgruntled fellow Marine grumbled, "They (meaning the military officers) just chew you up and then spit you out."

This encampment would mark a turning point in the climb. Before starting out again, the trio strapped spiked crampons to their boots and pulled thick nylon coverings over their upper boots and legs mid-calf for protection from the winds and to keep moisture from creeping into the inner layers. Joni's gaiters, as the leg coverings are called, were bright red, setting off the blues of her additional nylon gear.

Motorcycle Hill, for the next 1,000 feet of climbing, had a pronounced slope, much steeper than what they had encountered up to that time. The snow was no longer light and fluffy, but hard packed and at times encrusted with rocks. "I'd feel my way along so that I wouldn't stumble on the rocks," Joni stated afterward. "Fortunately my crampons stayed secure, but I still checked them."

Their ascent fell into a definite pattern; Mike played the part of the Sherpa, tinkling a brass bell as he went in the lead, Joni followed in the middle, and Marty gave directions from behind.   Marty, who seemed to have a sixth sense about the weather, related the meaning of the winds and cloud formations, and served as navigator. Frequently checking his compass in heavy fog or blowing snow, he kept the team on track. But for the most part, there were clear skies and they were able to follow the trail created by the other climbers.

Park rangers frequently passed by them, asking how they were doing or if they needed any help. Joni came to believe that they were being given special attention because of her blindness.

"I could tell she (Joni) was blind by the way she groped along, but then I already knew that she'd be on the mountain, commented Daryl Miller, a muscular Denali National Park Service mountaineering ranger. A climbing veteran whose light-brown hair is heavily peppered with gray, Miller had reached the McKinley summit numerous times since 1981 and had worked with physically challenged climbers in Colorado.   "It was easy to recognize them, especially with her tall twin son's huge, camouflaged backpacks.

"Other climbing teams stand out because of the violent disagreement between the members, especially those where people have been put together at random basis, hailing from cities around the world such as Seattle, New York, London and Frankfurt," said Miller. "(Even) Long-standing friendships are sometimes dissolved because of being constantly roped to each other," said Miller.

In contrast, the Phelps trio worked well together, but harmony among them wasn't absolute. When Joni stepped on the rope, Mike would shout at her like a drill sergeant giving his troops a reprimand. He knew that each misstep with the spiky crampons could damage the vital lines.

Joni suffered Mike's harsh words in silence, telling herself that he was right in yelling. Gentle Marty stepped in to make the orders more understandable, using his knack for teaching to explain the underlying dangers of frayed ropes. Even though they had brought along extras, every one might be needed in case of an emergency.

On the rare occasions when Joni allowed her mind to drift, it settled on the springtime that was unfolding at home in Pennsylvania. "What I missed most was the smells of flowers," she later said, sidestepping in her typical fashion any unpleasant references to the strong body fragrance the three "ripe" climbers soon developed, a consequence of their exertion and the primitive camping conditions. Her normally fluffy hair was flattened by the blue wool cap that protected her ears from frostbite and the constant wind.

As the mountain terrain grew more rugged, rest days between rigorous climbs became a necessity for Joni, to give her body time to recoup and to ensure the all-important adjustment to the increasing altitude. The trio decided not move on to to move until all three would be able to sleep at night, a signal that the body had become acclimated. Before she went to sleep, Joni would take aspirin and ibuprofen tablets to relieve the minor aches and pains she felt. Though they had agreed to admit if they were hurting, no one said very much about discomfort, even when Marty developed a burning bone blister on his hip from carrying both his pack and a portion of his mother's.

Mike and Marty, always ready to literally go the extra mile, carried gear ahead to each successive camp as Joni waited below in the tent. While the twins were off on one of these trips to move gear forward, Joni heard what sounded like thunder. At the time she didn't think much of it, but when Mike and Marty returned, they described the ferocity of an avalanche that had fallen like a collapsing 10-story building within about 100 yards of them.

The dangers of McKinley, which the men attempted to downplay to their mom, still came through loud and clear in their voices, especially when they cautioned that the risk factor would greatly increase beyond 14,000 feet. Joni turned as always to prayer for guidance for a safe climb and as a comforting way of protecting them from becoming part of the deadly statistics of McKinley: One in every 50 climbers perishes.

"When one of God's children makes it, there's rejoicing in heaven," these words of Reverend Andres, former minister of the First Church of the Nazarene in Warren during Joni's formative years, assured her that all of them were in the hands of God, and that he alone would decide the time for meeting their Maker in heaven.

Windy Corners

Temperature fluctuations during each day were met with the usual Phelps "be prepared" attitude. As the frigid air warmed at times to 50 degrees Fahrenheit, the team usually removed a few of their outer layers to prevent their inner clothing from becoming damp with sweat. Aware of their mother's lifelong susceptibility to frostbite, the boys were quick to insist that she put her extra jacket back on as soon as the temperature dipped even slightly downward.

Along the way, the twins drew a verbal picture of Mt. McKinley's powerful landscape as dwarfing even the Grand Canyon, a site Joni recalled seeing in awe-inspiring photographs in her elementary school textbooks. She could picture in her mind the white-capped mountain peaks and huge cornices as she felt the warm sun strike her during the day, heightening the drama of a scene cast in the never-ending sunlight of the Alaskan summer.

Taking the West Buttress route around Windy Corners at 13,200-feet elevation proved a challenge for Joni just as it had for Barbara Washburn when she became the first woman to climb Mt. McKinley in 1947. She pioneered the route with her husband, Bradford Washburn, who led "Operation White Tower," an expedition to map the mountain's peaks and valleys. The long ramps continued to get steeper as the Phelpses forged ahead. The winds from which the site took its name proved vicious, showing their strength by blowing away the snow in some places and in others leaving rocks as large as washtubs strewn on the hard-packed snow.

The team managed to climb another 1,000 feet upward from this well-known point where treacherous gusts can freeze exposed skin within minutes and bury climbers in mounds of snow. Fluorescent wands in the hard-packed snow showed them the way through squinting eyes when wind-blown particles dazed them.

The hidden crevasses and the jumble of rocks, like twisted roots on a forest floor, made it hard to walk, but Joni treasured the freedom of movement provided by the 50-foot lifeline connecting her to her sons. "We used three-way radios to keep in touch, but the best thing I could do was feel my way at this point. I focused on keeping stability, having my weight balanced over my feet and taking short breaths since the air seemed thinner the closer we got to the summit."

A Frenchman who followed the trio had careened into a crevasse the day before, saved only by his pack. The light aluminum framework and its bulky load of supplies became wedged in a small crevice and prevented his death.

The area where they camped that fourth night on the mountain was just beyond the ranger station which supplies the weather conditions on Mt. McKinley. It was situated on the leeward side of a flat expanse that had been probed for snow-covered crevasses. Fortunately with the weather station close by, an easy radio contact could be made if a problem occurred.

The next morning the twins dug a 3-foot hole to bury a cache and their two sleds, which would have been too difficult to haul throughout the rest of the climb. Marking the location with two 4-foot wands made of finger-sized bamboo with fluorescent orange tape affixed to the ends, the twins also made a mental note of the location. To ease the load in their mother's backpack, they still toted gear ahead to 16,000 feet, an interlude that meant an extra day's grace for Joni's exhausted body.

In a letter written from their camp site at 14,200 feet, Joni noted that few of the other climbers had figured out that she was blind. But as the climb became more difficult, the trio knew to be more concerned about safety than trying to fool other climbers into believing that Joni could see. Along with the greatly increased risk beyond this camp came greater physical challenges. Here was where the real climbing began, and the terrain became more spectacular.

On an entertaining note that speaks tellingly of the depths of the crevasses, the team amused themselves along the way by listening for the landing of personal waste. Mike would head to the edge of a crevasses and then dumped the odoriferous plastic bag used in place of a toilet, while Marty questioned, "Has it landed yet?"

"Not yet," responded Mike.

"Has it landed yet?"

"No, not yet."

"Has it landed yet?"

"Yes."

The longer it took to hit, the deeper the crevasse.

For all the humor the vast slots provided, these pits could be extremely hazardous as well. "This crevasse is big enough to swallow a large building," Marty said, describing a gigantic hole which dropped 50 feet down, a "slot" of mammoth proportions which lay between them and their goal. Joni began carefully navigating the edge of the crevasse, using her ski pole to feel her way in front and her ice ax to dig into the side surface of the mountain's face. Whenever the going got rough like this, the 50-foot lifeline linking her to the twins was shortened to just 15 feet to provide extra safety in negotiating the hazard.

As she baby stepped along, her foot slipped off the icy edge and she slid downward a few feet. "As I felt myself going over the side, I felt the security of the ropes holding me, the boys holding me," recalled Joni, reporting the incident more like a mildly eventful crossing of a road than a possible end to her life. "I rolled on my side, made a grip for myself and got back on the path while the boys gave me direction and told me to concentrate on my breathing."

THE WALL

Representing a true contest for Joni was the headwall of this majestic mountain. "To me, this wall seemed to rise straight up," she said of the area which most say is the crux of the climb. Even master mountaineers take this challenging wall very seriously. Its 50-degree angle put stress on every muscle in the body.

On the right-hand side of twin 1,000-foot ropes which had been permanently attached to the headwall by the McKinley park service to save climbers valuable time and afford added safety, Joni attached one of her two steel ascenders, commonly referred to as Jumars. These unique devices, when clipped to the rope, gave her protection and yet freedom because they were hand-controlled. When necessary, each gripped the rope, or it could be squeezed open to permit Joni to slide upward.

Bolstered by the double security from Mike and Marty's ropes and "fixed-pro," extra ice screws attached as they progressed, she wedged her crampons into the icy wall and pounded her ice ax into the glassy surface. Little by little she inched upward. At the 10 to 15 security stops called anchors, she managed to clip one Jumar before unclipping the other and calling out "Ready!" to the twins, but the procedure was excruciatingly slow.

"Going up that 800-foot ice wall went on forever," said Joni of the challenge. "It must be this goal that keeps you going ahead, and my faith says it's all right."

The higher the elevation, the more intense the cold became but the extra exertion needed to scale the wall caused all three to perspire at times. Still they kept forging ahead.   Within a day's climb, the trio had risen almost 2,000 feet.   Joni's nine months of training again provided the key to her success. The bench presses at the YMCA had developed the strong muscles needed to lift her wiry body toward the heavens.

In a rare window of opportunity, the unbelievable good weather continued to hold and the weather station predicted possibly two to three more sunny days. "Someone up above just had to be looking out for me," said Joni afterwards. "We were told this was the best weather in many years."

Camp 5 at 16,200 feet was setup on a narrow ledge less than 50 feet wide and within 1,000 feet in elevation from Summit City, the launching point for climbing to the apex of McKinley. The twins had hoped to make it all the way there before stopping, but they could tell by their mother's hesitant steps that she needed to rest.

Joni had known in advance how the climb would affect her body, having learned from the Braille cards she carried with her about the diarrhea, nausea and vomiting associated with altitude sickness; the affects of extremely dry, cold air; and special techniques of breathing. She was determined to maintain her internal balance and keep her blood oxygen levels up through slow steps while climbing and short breaths while sleeping.

For sons Mike and Marty, taking every precaution possible to ensure success had been a hallmark of their outdoor existence. They talked with a McKinley ranger about the minutest safety details, from all conceivable angles, and how to maximize the odds of a successful climb.

"The twins showed great love and fortitude for their mother," ranger Miller later commented. "They were receptive to advice and asked a lot of questions."

The weather continued to hold as the team took off the next morning for 17,200 feet elevation with plans of attempting the summit the following day. Climbing the additional 1,000 feet strained and seemed to weaken Joni's body. Such a reaction to the higher elevations proved a common problem for climbers of McKinley, according to ranger Miller who observed that Joni noticeably staggered as she trudged up the mountain from camp 5 on Friday, May 21.

"I was sore, but didn't dwell on it because I like to emphasize the positive," said Joni of the strain and peril along the way. "When thoughts of dying entered my mind, I didn't let them linger, and then everything was all right."

There were no unnecessary words spoken among the climbers, only silence, except for the crunching of each methodical step, the tinkle of the bell and a plain, commanding monologue, "Your next step is above your knee, pick up right foot, way up high."

Joni concentrated on her breathing and stayed focused, scaling a large outcropping of rock without incident. In fact, the climb had been remarkably free of mishaps, and none of the snow bridges on which their lives depended had collapsed. Joni credited this good fortune to a "guiding light" from above.

The team stopped along the way to have a light lunch, bagel sandwiches and flavored liquids, which had been their midday fare throughout the climb. Relishing the break, Joni took extra time to rest on a large rock before pitting her body once more against the physical rigors of Mt. McKinley.

The twins described a magnificent cornice of white sculptured curves, and they paused to photograph this towering piece of natural art created by the unique conditions of McKinley. Like so much of the mountain's magnificent landscape, this imposing but beautiful formation would have proven deadly if it had let loose and buried an adventurer in an icy grave.

The sight of Summit City, a broad and surprisingly level expanse that in lower altitudes might have been a mountain meadow, spotted first by Marty was a welcome relief. "Mom, you should see this area, it's like one big football field," he said of the seemingly never ending expanse of white.

The hard-packed snow made a strange squeaky crunch like Styrofoam as the trio explored the area for a spot to pitch their tent. Other climbing teams milled around, getting their bodies ready for their own assaults on the apex of Mt. McKinley. "Most of the other teams were foreigners, German and Japanese, " said Joni, who recognized the accents she heard from nearby tents. "We met a man from Seattle who was very friendly."

The trio practiced the short breaths needed to help regulate bodies used to lower altitudes. This camping area was the last because human beings cannot withstand for an extended period of time the altitude of the 20,320-foot summit. Even on a clear day, when the extensive 600-mile range of mountain peaks provides a stunning view that entices weary climbers to linger, remaining on top of the mountain could be fatal.

"I worried about safety beyond the jet stream, from

18,000 feet up to 20,000 feet," said Marty afterward. (At 18,000 feet above sea level, there's 50 percent less oxygen in the air than at sea level.)

At one corner of the Summit City basin is a famous snow cave, jokingly called "the Hilton," where climbers often take refuge from storms. But the relatively flat basin outside the cave would be protection enough and not be as cold as camping within its icy walls. Mike and Marty knew this "icebox" would be an unnecessary discomfort, too cold in the absence of the punishing winds of a horrendous storm.

Instead, they built a well-engineered protective wall and crouched within its shelter to plan what gear and supplies they would take to the top. They knew they had to travel with just the essentials to keep their loads light. There was the temptation to take everything, "just in case," but that would be foolhardy. The very things intended to safeguard their lives could cause their demise if the final drive was encumbered.

They knew extra protection, liquids and food were vital because of their mother's tendency toward frostbite and her decrease in energy at this challenging altitude. In case their mother needed to have an emergency shelter built, a shovel was a must as were radios and a sleeping bag. Even though they had learned that the rangers kept an emergency cache at the summit which contained medical supplies such as oxygen for climbers with severe breathing problems, as well as food, ropes and other safety equipment, the twins planned to carry extra ropes and food with them just in case there was a problem.

After a fitful night of sporadic sleep, they started on that first, unsuccessful attempt at the summit. After about 4 hours of arduous climbing and Joni's slip on the narrow ledge, the quest was ended. Their mom had been saved only by the ropes and the quick action of her sons, otherwise she would have descended into a 900-foot freefall, landing on the jagged rocks of the infamous "Jaws" crevasse. Even though they had traveled less than a mile to that point, every step had been a trial. Each time Joni had to contend with the urgent demand of the diarrhea, she needed to unclip the loops of the harness under her leg and drop the back flap of her insulated suit. Even this simple procedure taxed her exhausted body, and the exposure wracked her with chills.

Slowly and carefully they worked their way off this extremely dangerous ridge, which varied in width from 6 to 10 inches. Next the team traversed along an area with 30-to 45-degree slope downward. Even though they were descending, their muscles were tense yet fatigued at the same time. Every footsteps seemed to be made in slow motion, like a film projector caught at the wrong speed. The illusion, of course, was part fatigue and part regret over failure.

"You've covered the worst section of the whole mountain," the ranger's encouraging words echoed in the bonded trio's minds as they slowly and cautiously headed back to camp five at 16,400 feet elevation, which would give their mother's exhausted body a chance to rest. "...The most difficult terrain." Their resolve to control their minds and bodies intensified, and the set of the Phelpses' strong, inherited jaw line revealed their decision to succeed if another attempt became possible.

The tactic of temporarily retreating followed the advice of the McKinley guidebook, "Mountaineering," which offers climbers information vital to their safety and welfare. The book stated that many parties experiencing early signs of AMS have completed a successful expedition by descending 2,000 to 3,000 feet allowing for one or two days of acclimatization and then ascending again more slowly.

Chapter Eight

"To cry is to risk being too emotional..."

A PERILOUS CHALLENGE

Mammoth, billowing clouds on the ninth day developed endless peaks, signaling a dramatic change in the weather: a storm. The weather-wary Marty predicted it would hit by the end of the day's climb.

After more than a week of almost perfect weather conditions of beautiful sunshine and moderate breezes with the exception of gusty Windy Corners, suddenly the skies began to change. Joni understood that such a fluctuation was more typical of the mountain's unpredictable ways than the weather they had enjoyed thus far.

Even in late spring and throughout the summer, McKinley can throw a curve into the most experienced climbers' plans. Just a few hundred miles north of this majestic, dangerous peak is the Arctic Circle. Its capricious storms merge double-dealing winds and sub-zero temperature.

Returning to the area of Camp 5 at 16,400 feet elevation was not an ideal situation with a storm brewing, but Joni needed to regain her strength. The team had no choice if they wanted to succeed. Fortunately, they had camped once more on the leeward side, where there was less wind and greater protection. However, the twins knew that with the impending storm, an extra fortified "bomber-proof" wall, a mountaineering term coined in World War II to describe a well-built structure, would have to be constructed around the tent.

Joni carved snow blocks with a snow knife, helping to create a 5-foot barrier which protected them from the 80-mph gale. "Carve bottom side, insert left, insert right," said Joni recalling the process. "When they asked me to pick it up, I was amazed at the light weight of a snow block."

Referring to their down sacks, good to minus 40 degrees, she continued, "I'm sure the temperature dropped to a least 30 degrees below zero at night, since our highly insulated sleeping bags were chilly when we awoke. We survived the cold easily within our protected tent."

With Joni's weakened state and slip into the "Jaws" crevasse, the trio seriously questioned whether they could make it. Did they have the physical endurance, and even more importantly the cerebral strength, to make the summit without endangering their lives? Would they have to turn back like so many other climbers, satisfied only in the fact that they had tried?

"Blessed is the name of the Lord," these words seemed to surround them within the confines of their tent. That night they prayed together, broke bread and asked once more for guidance on their perilous journey. All three acknowledged looking forward to heaven and eternity together as they placed themselves in God's care. Their bodies seemed to recuperate with a night's sleep, and a moderate morning meal bolstered their energy to go forward.

A look outside their tent, however, showed 10 inches of new snow and zero visibility. Instead of only one day of rest at this point, the trio's encampment proved a four-day bivouac inside the small, three-person tent, but the team was prepared. They were aware that a storm like this could wipe out everyone, a prospect that could take the starch out of even the most experienced mountaineers.

Disagreements, as deadly to morale and the success of the climb as an avalanche, trumpeted from nearby tents, where climbers seemed to be at odds over seemingly basic issues. Meshing four to six unknown personalities created extreme tension and made Joni thankful they were climbing Mt. McKinley as a family team.

"We read books to each other, visited other climbers also held up by the storm," she later recalled.

"We put more time into food preparation and ate extra-fancy trail-pack meals such as beef stroganoff and lasagna." When in Warren, Joni always had attempted to maintain her weight at about 135 to 140 pounds by eating sparingly at times, but on the mountain her appetite flagged and she had to force herself to consume enough calories just to maintain her energy.

"There was always something puttery to do," she explained afterwards. "I rearranged my felt inner sole for extra warmth or put a button on a jacket. The boys were continually rebuilding the wall.

"When the boys disagreed, Marty would just leave, which would frustrate Mike. Each one wanted the other to be just like him," said Joni of the tension between the two. Personality differences continued to arise between the bonded twins, just as they had throughout their rambunctious childhood.

Even with this forced solitude, they tried to save their breath and strength, however, concentrating on remaining focused on their goal. What amazed Joni was that this storm, just like the one before they started, made a positive difference. Instead of posing an obstacle in her climb, it served as a welcome relief, giving her body time to adjust once more to the thinner air.

When the storm finally passed, 40 inches of new snow encased their tent in a mantle of white. Joni placed gear out in the afternoon sunshine and brisk winds to dry. Being enclosed in their small tent during the storm had caused even their sleeping bags to feel damp from the condensation of their breath.

A quietness had pervaded the mountain. The din of the wind no longer filled Joni's ears, making concentration difficult. It seemed as if the weather was an ornery child that had been calmed by outside forces. At times, voices echoed in the distance, and Joni wondered if they were angels. Because of the heavy snow, they strapped on basketweave-style snowshoes. These prevented them from sinking in too deep as they trudged the 1,000 feet upward and proceeded to once again set up camp at the famous "football field."

Mom of the Mountain

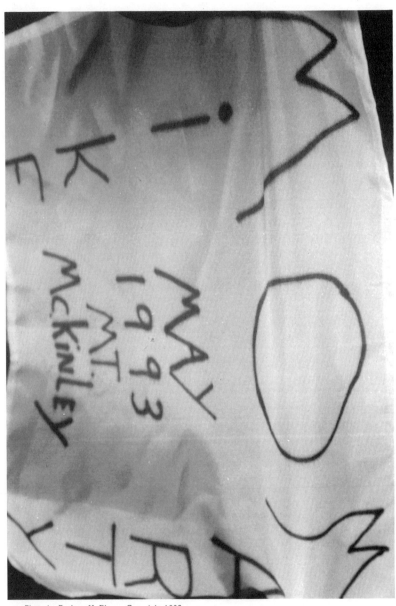

Photo by Barbara N. Ekey, Copyright 1993

Chapter Nine

"To laugh is to risk being a fool..."

TOP OF THE WORLD

With a relatively good night's rest at their second Summit City camp, the team had a light breakfast, minus the beans that Joni blamed for the diarrhea that stymied their first attempt. The weather was perfect, sunny with a comparatively light breeze.

At around 11:00 a.m. on Sunday, May 30, 1993, the intently focused team, tethered with a 15-foot security rope, crunched the rock-hard surface of what climber's affectionately call the "autobahn." As the trio systematically stepped upward, Mike's brass bell played the lead and Marty's baritone voice provided direction from behind. The three bonded climbers were determined to succeed in this last attempt at setting a world record.

Joni controlled her physical needs and attuned her

breaths and steps to the internal signals of her body as they moved up the gentle slope which began the day's climb. Fortunately, there were no rocks over which to stumble, but running protection (placing of movable ice screws into the snow wall) soon was needed as the angle steepened to 30 to 45 degrees. Each with his or her right foot against the slope, the trio inched along.

"I knew I could make it if I stayed focused," Joni later commented about the harrowing final assault. A lifetime of determined action against physical restrictions came into play, her positive psychological state willing her body to respond to her mind's desire.

After less than a mile of climbing — but 600 feet higher in elevation — the ledge narrowed to about 6 inches at 17,800 feet elevation with the deadly "Jaws" crevasse below. This familiar, extra treacherous quarter-mile section still lay between them and the top, presenting a seemingly endless challenge.

Could they surmount this formidable hazard?

Mike and Marty again gave themselves "fixed protection" by putting pickets into the wall, limiting to an even greater extent any misstep or fall.

Halfway across this deadly face, just as it seemed likely that they would succeed, climbers coming from the opposite direction put panic in their hearts. Worrying about how to get them to go around without risking the life of their mother struck horror into Mike and Marty's hearts. "We weren't very polite at all," Mike said of the encounter. "We weren't moving. I didn't like it at all"

After making the oncoming climbers understand their mother was blind, all three dug their ice axes into the sidewall and hugged the surface. The descending adventurers inched first around on the outside of Mike, then Joni and finally Marty. The descenders' feet came within an inch of slipping off the ledge where Joni had slipped before, an inch from plummeting 900 feet into the gigantic maw.

For Mike and Marty, it was the most difficult

moment of the climb, they both said later. "Our options were limited and we had to stand our ground," explained Marty. "To retreat again would really be testing fate, and as always, Mom's safety was paramount."

The challenges were not all behind them, however. The mountain rose further skyward on the far side of the ledge. Even though it had already taken 4 hours, the day's climb wasn't even halfway completed. Next they slowly and painfully ascended to the Denali Pass where the West Buttress meets Harper Glacier. Since the skies were clear and there was a relatively light wind, the adventurers took a few minutes to rest. Though weary from the exhausting climb, they decided to go ahead, certain that if they continued to climb a step at a time they could make it. For many climbers this spot proved the turn-around point, the place where the summit finally was accepted as an impossibility.

Fortunately, the white, car-size granite boulders sporadically scattered across the compressed surface in the next section didn't seem to impede their progress as they muddled along the windy trail. Without seeing it, Joni had passed Archdeacon's Tower, a 200-foot-high buttress on the left hand side, its granite polished smooth by centuries of savage winds.

After conjuring up extra strength for Denali Pass with its 20 to 30 degree angle, the twins told their mother, "Up ahead is a big football field." What they were describing was a 100 yard area at 19,600 feet above sea level with a mostly flat surface, but where no footballs had ever been thrown. An exertion of that type would have been impossible; just tightening the straps of the crampons or lifting a foot over a rock required a formidable effort.

The trick to climbing the last leg up to the peak of McKinley was to maintain a precarious balance, going fast enough not to get too cold, but slowly enough to be able to breath. Joni's tendency toward frostbite made the balance more tenuous, worrying her sons.

After 10 hours into the arduous climbing, the team reached an icy incline with a 35 to 40 degree angle. The hard-packed snow steps were uneven, which made Joni's breathing irregular and threw her footsteps out of rhythm. She reached into the deepest wells of her inner strength, dragging herself forward. She make sure to take a split-second halt between each step, giving her muscles and body a moment to recover from the stress and tension.

Excruciating as it was, each step confirmed in Joni's mind that she could make it, that she could climb to the apex of her desires, overcoming the freezing thin air that seemed at times to be almost devoid of life-giving oxygen. The final test was the summit ridge, just a quarter mile, but exposed to the full force of the wind. With the temperature at a minus 20 degrees Fahrenheit and the added wind chill factor, it felt like at least 30 degrees below zero to the exhausted climbers.

On May 30, 1993, after having dangled their bodies before the mouths of crevasses, enduring uncertainty and confinement, and finally willing their spent limbs to scale this difficult icy incline, the adventurers reached the zenith of their dreams. In Alaska's golden midnight sun, 11 hours after they had started the ultimate assault, Joni Phelps stood on a prow-shaped mound of snow, removed her glove and waved to the unseen world stretched out beneath her.

As the three held one of the two small flags they had brought, with "MOM" across the top horizontally, interlocked with Mike and Marty written vertically, Joni felt keenly the intense cold, the clarity of the air and the radiance of the sun, to which she had never been closer in her life. Her body, which for days had been weighed down by worries and fatigue, suddenly felt light. She savored the moment through her sons' descriptions of the stunning panorama of McKinley's summit of clear skies and jagged, lesser peaks.

"The view from the top of the world was incredible, a truly inspirational experience," Joni later related.

"According to the boys, you could see forever."

From the south face, which drops 8,000 to 10,000 feet straight down, a window of good weather allowed for a clear view of Mount Hunter and Mount Forker. But the climbers' plan was to limit their time at the summit to less than 5 minutes, including the shooting of a few historic photos. "We didn't stay at the summit very long," commented Marty afterwards. "I was worried about the climb back down."

Another seven hours of possibly even more difficult climbing and definitely more dangerous stepping brought the triumphant trio back to Summit City. The crunch of the snow was interrupted by the sound of a helicopter on another "practice mission," or so the twins would have liked their mother to believe. With intense concentration and without interference they had navigated their tired, exhausted bodies safely back across that narrow ledge which had put fear into their souls and threatened to rob them of their moment of supreme achievement. Just before reaching 17,200 feet they saw ranger Miller and gave him a thumbs up signal that they had made the summit.

Though bleary from the grueling 18-hour round trip of their second assault on the summit, the trio maintained their hyper state of concentration. "Back at camp there was a lot of celebration, but not the boys. They were concerned about my frostbitten fingers (from taking off her glove to wave) and getting the stove warm for melting snow for hot drinks," said Joni, who became painfully aware of her natural tendency toward frostbite. "I warmed my hands by putting them under my armpits and crawled into my sleeping bag for warmth and rest."

What she did not mention in her retelling of their triumphant return was the commotion caused by the death of Joni's acquaintance from Seattle. Newspaper reports told of the death of Charlie Cearly, age 40, who was killed at 11:00 p.m. on May 30, 1993, about one hour after the Phelpses reached the McKinley Summit. While descending another McKinley route called the Orient Express, he slipped and catapulted 3,000 feet down, about the distance of three Empire State Buildings. The helicopter attempting to rescue him would have been heard by all three of the tired climbers, but all that Joni later lamented was that "He was unroped, so there was nothing to stop his fall."

The threesome ended their eventful day by once again praying together. Joni, still warming her fingertips, put a special balm on her sunburned lips and fell into a well-deserved sleep. Only her short, trained breaths or the occasional noisy inhaling of Marty or Mike disturbed the moment of perfect peace.

Chapter 10

"To express one's feelings is to risk expressing your true self..."

A DISCONCERTING DESCENT

By the next morning Joni's fingertips, no longer pink with telltale spots of white in the center, had returned to their normal color. "As I examined them, I hoped I didn't have any permanent damage," she said, a thread of worry entering her mind that their achievement would entail unpredictable anguish.

The two days spent moving back down the mountain would indeed cause Joni great drama and misery. She had lost her focus and longed to be back in Anchorage, only 130 air miles south, or better yet, taking a springtime walk through the Pennsylvania woods with her husband. The forests would be cloaked in green, she knew, and filled with the beautiful songs of nesting birds and the fragrance of flowers. She would be freed of the harsh realities of the climb, which on her ran roughshod over her usual instance of focusing on good, pleasant and positive things. Once back home, she could block out the ignoble agony of chronic diarrhea and share with Stan and friends the glossed-over glory of her achievement with her sons.

More serious thoughts were demanded by their circumstances, however. They knew that 80 percent of the 76 deaths on McKinley to date, Cearly's among them, occurred as climbers made their way down, according to Ranger Miller. Many of these tired adventurers, though mostly roped, somehow missed minor safety precautions that could have saved their lives. Of those who died the season preceding the Phelpses' climb, one was from the United States with four from Canada, three from Korea, two from Italy and one from Austria.

To make doubly sure of safety for their own descent, the Phelps party developed a new walking pattern with both Joni and Mike holding onto the same ski pole. A gentle motion from Mike directed his mother, making their progress simpler and swifter. This method was necessitated by the change in the terrain. On the way up Joni had put most of her weight on the fronts of her boots, but if she did that on the way down, she would have fallen forward. Feeling the direction indicated by the pole freed Joni to concentrate on putting her weight on the heels of her boots, digging in as best she could as they slowly trekked down the mountain.

Accustomed as she had grown to a sense of the mountain rising before her, Joni worried about the change. She might fall forward, she thought, or even worse drop into one of the numerous crevasses which had opened due to the warm weather that followed the big storm. Would this be the snow bridge which would collapse as she crossed? she'd ask herself.

To keep her mind off the danger facing her sons and her own personal peril, Joni started to envision how she would rearrange the furniture at home. "I re-did the living room, moving around the chairs, tables and lamps," she later said with a far-off tone, as if even in recollection of the troubling descent, she had set herself in another world.

An almost entertaining relief presented itself when Joni reached the headwall, which fortunately wasn't backed up with climbers as Miller says it often is in fair weather. Going down the steep cliff was like an amusement park ride as she deftly slid along the fixed rope using her Jumar as a grip and a brake. Every 60 feet, she'd yell "Anchor!" as she stopped to first clip her other Jumar to the next section and then unclip from the previous rope. "It was like rappelling in college," Joni commented afterwards. "I slid down with ease."

At 14,000 feet the trio pitched their tent for the last time. With the breathing easier now due to the lower elevation and their bodies reacting with an almost euphoric sense of relief, the triumphant team slept through the night. On June 2, before setting out on their last downward challenge, the twins found their cache marked by the brightly decorated wands. (McKinley stories circulated that if the cache had not been buried deep enough, hungry ravens had been known to dig it up for a gluttonous feast.) The pair also checked in with the ranger station and retrieved their sleds.

On their final day Joni carried very little in her backpack, but Mike and Marty, with faces well-tanned from the continuous sun and wind, persisted in pulling the sleds with the extra gear, minus the food they had eaten. Bringing back all the gear was their idea, a way of saving the equipment for future adventures.

This last day proved to be another 18-hour marathon, long in more ways than one. When the sled which Mike pulled careened into a large crevasse, landing 50 feet down in its frozen hole Joni froze in unaccustomed fear when Mike immediately exclaimed, "I'll get it."

Leaving their mother at a safe distance from the danger, Mike and Marty set out to use the skills they had learned during their training classes. As soon as Marty provided fixed protection by putting in pickets and ice screws, Mike rappelled down into the icy crypt. No mother wants to experience the desolate possibilities of something like that.

Perhaps it was fatigue or the relaxed attitude she had slipped into as the climb neared its end, but for the first time, Joni felt terror grab at her heart, an uncontrollable panic that something might happen to her twin sons. She tried to put the pieces of her shattered composure back together, an exercise like her quilting, but the tormenting worry for her twins' safety gripped her mind. What if Mike gets buried in the crevasse and Marty is unable to rescue him? Worse yet, what if both get entombed in the same gaping hole?

Grasping as she often did for a familiar comfort, she prayed out loud. "God, please protect my sons." She wished she could be the one to be going after the sled, or even more so that the boys would have just forgotten about the sled, leaving it forever in its icy grave.

"We got it!" they said in unison from about 50 feet away. To her relief, the boys had managed to rescue the sled without any complications, returning to their worried mother with smiles on their faces that could offer her no consolation.

During all the dangers which Joni had faced while conquering Denali and satisfying her own personal quest, she lost command of her emotions just this one time, when she felt her boys were in danger. Only that concern and love of her sons could totally break her focus.

As the day extended into the evening hours, all three were exhausted, but especially Joni, who felt threatened by her emotional fears for the twins safety. Her focus never seemed to be regained. Bringing the danger back into her mind was another roped-saving of her body from disaster when she sunk up to her knees into a slot which had opened up.

"This snow bridge is about three yards long," said Marty of one of the many challenges created by the warm weather. Joni carefully crossed the link to safety, managing to follow Mike's tug of the pole. Even her body ached as she longed to be safely off the mountain.

"It seemed as if we were lost, that somehow we had taken a wrong turn. Marty radioed ahead, but we received a blurred signal," said Joni. "In my mind the direction we were heading was all wrong. We were lost, and Marty didn't tell me anything, just continued to downplay the problem."

"Don't worry, Mom," he said with tenderness. "I know where we are on the map."

Joni was beginning to understand why Heartbreak Hill had gotten its name. Her exhausted mind was playing games on her as she headed up the incline to base camp.

When the worn-out trio reached the 7,000-foot

base camp, they didn't even bother putting up a tent. All they could do was climb into their sleeping bags for needed rest. The next day "Annie" had a plane pick them up at their final resting spot.

News of Joni Phelps' successful climb flashed around the world. "Unseen steps tame McKinley, 1st blind woman summits Denali" headlined newspapers across North America. From Boston to Los Angeles, people relished the story about a woman being first in the world, just as they had when Joni's idol, Amelia Earhart, flew solo across the Atlantic. Even the national Examiner carried a center photo and story, testament to her achievement's broad appeal.

Similar to what the remarkable Amelia Earhart had done, Joni had pitted herself against the great odds and ultimately achieved distinction in the public arena with the assistance of her twin sons. This athletic, middle-aged woman's spiritual and physical feat became even more outstanding when viewed against the backdrop of her lifestyle. She certainly didn't fit the stereotypical image; an upper-middle class male who sees mountain climbing as a man's sport.

Research by the National Park Service and others produced no question that Joni Phelps scored a first with her climb of the tallest mountain in North America. "After having searched our records, it looks as if Joni Phelps is the first blind individual to reach the summit of Mt. McKinley," Ranger Miller reported.

In fact, the exploits of only one other blind climber, Sir Francis Campbell, had gained widespread recognition. The famous educator considered reaching the pinnacle of Mont Blanc to be one of the crowning achievements of his life.

"Mont Blanc is nothing compared to McKinley," said Ranger Miller. "McKinley is the worst of the worst, a prolonged agony which is magnified by extreme weather conditions, but offset by the magnificent view from the top."

Joni flew back to Warren, greeted at the airport by her husband and guide dog Shear Pleasure. The reunion was recorded by TV camera crews who had heard of her world record through the Associated Press wire service. Even in the midst of the publicity blitz, plans and preparation for her next escapade, a marathon bike trip throughout England with friends from Ski for Light would quickly become her new focus.

Ironically in the face of the acclaim, Joni had roller-coasted from the highest pinnacle to the lowest ebb of her life.

From the Darkness of Retinitis Pigmentosa
to the
Golden Sunlight of Mt. McKinley's Summit!

Chapter Eleven

"To live is to risk dying....."

TWIN SEARCH

Even on the drive back to Anchorage, Mike and Marty were planning for their own next challenge. The triumph of McKinley somehow started to fade almost immediately into the background and their need for further adventure had become paramount.

What the bonded pair of highly trained adventurers chose as a follow-up was to search for Dall sheep in the southeastern finger of the 12,318,000-acre Wrangell-St. Elias National Park and Preserve. Located in eastern Alaska, some 250 miles from their home in Anchorage, it attracted a select group of mostly wealthy hunters. Their main objective was again to go where few had ever gone before: together, doing what they enjoyed most in life, exploring nature to the fullest. The dangers posed by chasing sheep along Barnard Glacier's volatile rim was something the brothers took in stride. They had hunted together since they had reached age 12, the legal minimum in Pennsylvania.

Two days after celebrating their birthdays and Christmas 1975 at the same time, the eager twins went hunting with their father for small game in the snow-covered Allegheny hills of their Pennsylvania home. Each shot straight and true, bringing home two rabbits for their mother to cook. This success motivated the brothers to range ever further afield in search of bigger and more elusive quarry.

Many times there was peril, but because they hunted together, they overcame the danger and later reveled in their success. Timing of their 1993 summer hunting adventure had been difficult due to conflicting work schedules and the pressing demands of the construction of their log home. This next ultimate hunting adventure had been postponed two times.

Mike had an opportunity to reflect on these delays as he lay within the frigid darkness of an icy crypt he thought might become his last resting place. Trapped by a crushing mound of ice that had fallen away from the face of the glacier as he walked beneath it, he faced the possibility that the seemingly endless seasons of the twins' quest might come to an end. Hoping to have his brother rescue him once again from disaster, Mike yelled repeatedly, "Mart, Mart, I need help!" Questions started to race through his mind: Can't he hear me? Why isn't he coming?

On Monday, Aug. 16, the rugged partners were on the forth day of a 10-day hunting trip on Alaska's remote Barnard Glacier, stalking the surreally rugged landscape for rams with fully curled horns. The hunt was proceeding as planned. An especially large ram had filled the lens of their spotting scope the previous day; when, without warning, the overhanging ice wall gave way with a groan, dropping mammoth ice boulders as the hunters walked beneath it.

Luckily, Mike had been flung into a small crevice when the glacier's overhang calved or collapsed. The full force of the ice had smashed against his aluminum frame backpack, wrapping it around his body like a pretzel. He did a quick damage survey of his body and discover that only the ankle he'd already weakened during a basketball game in June seemed to hurt.

The strapping 6-foot 2-inch outdoorsman needed help dislodging the weighty chunks that enveloped him, but he wanted his brother to know he was all right.

"Mart, Mart, I'm all right! I'm trapped at the base of the wall." Mike called again and again, but heard nothing from his brother. He started to assess the situation: he just might be able to get out of this cold, dark tomb alive, he thought, and then laugh about the predicament later with Marty.

He tried to ease his body forward, but a chunk of ice blocked his way. Then he spotted a glimmer of light down by his feet. Squirming slowly in that direction, maneuvering out of the frame of his pack in the process, he edged through a small opening in the jumble of ice.

What the relieved adventurer discovered upon getting out terrified him. His brother hadn't responded because he couldn't. A huge heap of gravel-laced boulders of ice had fallen with incredible force right where Marty had been walking, about 10 feet further out from the ice wall.

"I was scared. The icy boulders were piled several feet high," Mike said later, tears welling in his eyes. As he tried to move one of the half-ton chunks that buried his brother, Mike thought that maybe he could dig him out. He'd have to risk going back into the crevice that saved his life to get his pack and a chopper. It was risky, but he had to help his brother.

After wriggling in and retrieving his gear, Mike

ferociously chopped at the icy boulders covering his twin, his mighty strokes scarcely penetrating the outer edges. His mind racing, he surveyed the heap, trying to mentally visualize where he had last seen his brother compared to his own ice burial.

"He must be right here," he thought as he chose a new spot and started to dig with renewed hope, but again he was unable to dislodge the piano-sized barriers.

To make the situation more urgent, looming right over him was a massive slab of ice some 30 feet tall. The glacial calving that had trapped him and still held his twin brother had caused a new sheet of ice to move forward. If the glacier moved forward once again due to the melting in the 40-degree summer temperatures of midday, he would again be buried in ice. "It was almost like God was preventing me from reaching Mart," Mike said reverently.

After struggling for over an hour, he realized he would never free Marty alone. Yelling "Mart, Mart" several more times in parting, he set off over the thick white ice in the direction of their camp. His throbbing ankle went barely noticed, even though the initial injury had prevented him from running with Marty and his younger brother in the Crow Pass, a 28-mile cross-country Alaskan marathon in June.

"I knew I had to get help, but leaving him was the most difficult thing I've ever done in my life," said Mike, who had left all their food provisions on a rock in case, by miracle, Marty got free.

"Marty has been more than a brother to me," said Mike. "He was always there to help me no matter what." For almost three decades, the twins had been soul mates, best friends and constant companions. Before the hunting trip, Marty had just finished sanding the floors of their two-story log home, newly built of Sitka spruce, the state tree of Alaska.

As he headed the mile back to their camp, Mike kept shouting, "Mart, Mart." When he arrived at the spot where the brothers had slept side by side the previous night and discussed in their tent the trophy-sized ram they had spotted, he moved all the gear to the ice and placed the warmest sleeping bag, stove, lighter fluid and other survival items on a bright blue plastic tarp. In the center of the tarp, he made a large X out of fluorescent orange tape to send a distress signal to any planes which might fly over the area.

Remembering the escape plan he had created in his mind during the 15-minute flight in from the cabin where their hunt began, Mike started to walk across the ice in a westerly direction with his backpack filled with a tent, an ice pick, ropes and just enough provisions to survive. An instant of hope for rescue occurred when a small plane appeared in the distance.

"It didn't see me," he said, his eyes again filling with tears. "In fact, I even had my flag from the tent, and it was waving in the wind."

With grief and the intently focused determination

which had been the cornerstone of guiding their mother to McKinley's summit, Mike began what later was calculated by the National Park Service as a 20-mile hike over treacherous terrain. "I headed to the landing strip where we had planned on being picked up in ten days, hoping beyond hope that even though we had been out only four days, that they'd be making an early check on us," he said.

When he found the empty strip, he formed an S.O.S. out of rocks and started downstream in the direction of the cabin, where he knew he could get help to save his brother.

Traversing the rugged landscape with its extremely difficult moraine, he crossed swamps and bogs, and climbed over 10-high boulders and other irregular masses of glacial matter. At around 12:30 a.m. on Tuesday, he forded the rushing Chiltina River, at one time plunging up to his neck in a hole filled with frigid glacial run-off. The effect of the icy cold water quickly perpetrated his body and seemed to numb even his mind, but fortunately the water pushed him onto a rock where he could climb to safer ground.

Wet and worried about hypothermia, he felt lucky to have the tent with him. His unfeeling but experienced hands managed to set up the shelter, and he crawled inside, removed his wet clothing and tried to rest. "I prayed for God's help," said Mike simply.

The light of the next day brought renewed strength. After crossing a stream that had branched into five channels, he was "really cruising," covering ground swiftly as he moved along its gravel bars. "We can save Mart, we can save Mart," echoed in his mind and kept him going, knowing he was on target in his plan of rescue, thinking that he was doing just as Marty would have done.

Twelve hours into his limping race for help, Mike came to two trees interrupting the desolate landscape and felt elated to see the bright blue tin roof of the friend's lodge. His weak but urgent call immediately brought three guides running from the log structure, and they listened intently as Mike breathlessly related the critical danger of his brother.

Within moments, all four hopped into a plane heading for a camp from which they could radio for help. Because Mike was unfit to travel further, the guides flew on to the disaster scene and left him at the radio to direct the rescue over the airwaves. A C1 chopper of the National Park Service, paratrooper rescue team and refueling plane quickly responded to his radio S.O.S. and flew to the spot on the glacier marked with the bright X, near the place here Marty lay beneath the ice.

Mike's well-honed descriptive abilities had created a picture of the exact location of where his brother was trapped beneath the ice. By 11:30 a.m. on Tuesday, August 17, the glacial rescue was fully under way.

"It was so encouraging when everyone came to

help," said Mike, who had been told to remain in the cabin to recover from his grueling mission for assistance, "All I could do was sit down and pray for Mart and my family."

After five hours of searching in the dangerous shadow of the glacier's calving face, the experienced rescue teams had not found Marty Phelps. "I was the one who pronounced Marty dead," said Daryl Miller, the same National Park Service ranger who had talked with the climbing trio on Mt. McKinley. "It had been over 24 hours, and there was no way that Marty was alive under those huge, house-sized chunks. There was a high risk of other ice breaking off, and it was impossible to work in these life-threatening conditions. I doubt we'll ever find the body, since the ice floe went right under the glacier."

When the search was halted, the emotionally strung-out Mike was taken by helicopter to Providence Hospital in Anchorage for treatment of the ankle injury. After full body x-rays, he was released.

Before leaving the hospital, however, he called his parents in Pennsylvania to relate the tragic news about Marty. His stunned siblings flew into the Warren area from distant locations; his older sister Judy, a teacher, and her husband came from Massachusetts and his younger brother, Jim, from North Carolina.

Accompanied by Bruce Parker, a hunting and fishing guide and friend of both brothers, Mike also flew home to Warren where his and Marty's adventurous lives had begun within a few minutes of each other 29 years before.

A
new
challenge of
portentous proportion!

Chapter 12

"Amazing Grace how sweet the sound..."

GOLDEN REFLECTIONS

Joni hugged her lone twin Mike, and he in return intertwined his arms in hers. To many of the friends and family gathered at the modern brick First Church of the Nazarene in Warren for the service memorializing Marty J. Phelps on Saturday evening, August 12, it seemed as if their bonded arms served as a conduit of inner strength from mother to son and back again. Without their shared support, how could they endure the relentless pain of loss or manage to celebrate what their faith told them was Marty's glorious arrival in heaven?

In her 54 years, Joni Phelps had surmounted other tests of her deep-seated spiritual strength. Even when her own life had been imperiled on Mount McKinley, her belief in God's protective power had been unshaken.

Only on the way down, when her sons were in danger, had she wavered. Now that her worst fears were realized and her gentle, Christ-like son had been taken, she faced the supreme test.

Joni had grown up and established her home in this small rural community, where she and her husband Stan raised and educated four children with minimal financial flexibility. She instilled in them her spirituality, adventurous spirit, trust and willingness to take calculated risks, all of which enabled her twin sons to serve as her sighted guides on Mt. McKinley.

Her special vision, that ability to sense the essence of people and situations while most others seemed fixed on outward image, played a paramount role in her success, putting her on an equal footing and in comradeship with the world. With the birth of twin sons less than two years after bringing her daughter into the world, Joni had begun to recognize her capacity for mental and physical discipline. She learned to control her immediate surrounding through the rigors of double feedings and multiple diaper changes. Though immersed in the mundane, she had encouraged the children to seek out their dreams.

Joni frequently quoted the ending of her favorite poem: "BUT RISK YOU MUST— Because the greatest hazard to life is to risk nothing. He who risks nothing, does nothing, has nothing, is nothing. He may avoid suffering but he simply cannot learn, feel, change, grow, love, live. Chained by his certitudes, he is a slave; he has forfeited freedom. Only the person who risks, can he be called a free man."

With this strong belief, she had been no armchair adviser. Joni lead the way and pushed herself to the limits by confronting physical challenges and competitive opportunities. Even before McKinley she had claimed the silver medal in international cross-country skiing competition and shared with others her joy of living a full life. The story of her achievements inspired others to conquer their own personal barriers.

Joni and Stan had felt great pride when their children had accepted the Lord as their savior. She knew the significance of abiding faith as over the years, when worry had consumed her, Joni had retreated to her special relationship with the Lord, putting her total trust in his judgment. Now, she felt, for some unknown reason, the Lord had called Marty home.

As the church became more and more crowded and the balcony filled, Joni kept her attention centered straight ahead and her arms wrapped around Mike. "Dearly beloved, we are gathered together to pay a tribute of respect to Marty John Phelps...," said the dark-haired Reverend G.A. Hankins with a deep voice filled with emotion. "We don't understand and can't find answers to our questions...," he continued as if speaking aloud the thoughts of grief-stricken Joni.

In the front of the church stood an easel with a photo Marty had taken of himself when buck hunting in

Alaska. His handsome face glowed as he held the antlers of the deer he had just shot. Carved into the antique oak frame which surrounded the portrait were a series of indentations, as if a bear had clawed it; a touch Marty would have liked. The frame's craftsmanship was also fine, the sort his skilled hands could have replicated.

Standing alone, the mere shadow of the life it poignantly represented, the portrait took the place of a casket within the altar railing. Marty's body still hadn't been found. He was buried in a natural resting place selected by God, his body forever lying preserved in an icy Alaskan crypt.

A eulogy would seem almost a redundant summing up of his life, which he packed with compassion, concern and kindness in gestures large and small. Worried about his father's health, Marty had called just before leaving on the fateful hunting trip and urged Stan to put his trust in the Lord. He wanted, too, to plan their fall hunt in Alaska, letting his father know that he and Mike would provide for the airplane ticket. That was like Marty.

He felt compassion for the unfortunate souls, the "unlovables." He made everyone feel they could succeed with the help of faith. Now, Marty was with the Lord. He had lived a life in God's outdoor playground of Alaska, his physical strength, character and courage shining forth as he explored the unknown, living life to the fullest.

Testimony of Marty's influence and power came forth loud and clear as his friends and family extolled the remarkable effect he'd had on their lives and on the lives of others. This was a true "Victory for Jesus," just as the Calvary Singers sang. These singing friends had supported Joni through the joy of her McKinley success and now threw their hearts and voices into uplifting her at Marty's funeral.

"We're going to miss Marty.....," the minister continued. No one felt it more than his mother who had learned to rely on the young man's thoughtful words of encouragement. When on McKinley, the gentle twin healed the wounds made by Mike's harshly stated words, somehow making everything all right, making it possible for Joni to reach for her time in the molten, golden light of McKinley's apex. She treasured that moment knowing full well that without Marty and Mike, her matched pair of guides, she never would have made the summit and that few, if any, would be able to follow behind her.

Throughout life the twins had seemed almost like a single unit, but the tug between them had always been a subtext, with Mike wanting Marty to be just like him and not understanding his brother's need for independence. Ironically, right after Marty's death, Mike said many times that he wanted to be more like the caring, loving, giving Marty; a person who was more concerned with the needs of other's than of his own. Marty would happily give Mike the best sleeping bag and his choice of sleeping location as in the tent during the McKinley climb, but when another's feeling were involved, Marty stood his ground. This behavior frustrated Mike, who up until Marty's death could not understand the selflessness that caused his twin to take some one else's part against him.

With a jolt, Mike was initiated into the world of one. No longer would he have his brother to act as the other side of the coin. Suddenly he was his only resource, and from here, beginning with the collapse of the glacial wall, he'd be tested alone. Mike showed added tenderness as his muscular arms drew his mother a little closer to him.

Deep within herself Joni retained that sense of joy and peace that rested on the rock of her faith. But for the time being it was hidden by the pain of losing Marty. Like the winds of Denali, her control seemed to come and go. One look at Mike's anguished face told the same story. Would he be able to reconcile his pain and start to rebuild his life, for the first time without Marty as his constant companion?

"Please, oh Lord, transform this darkness into the

lightness of day..." Even when Joni lost her vision from retinitis pigmentosa, deep-seated faith represented a small window that remained slightly open, enlightening her darkened world and freeing her of the constraints of blindness to live a life of worth and adventure. Her vision, robbed by an inherited condition of its physical aspect, was enriched on a spiritual plane.

"Marty was prayed up...," the words floated through the air. Joni knew the words were true. Every night in their small, three-person tent, Mike, Marty and Joni had prayed together for guidance, just as when the boys were small, that old familiar prayer ending with, " If I die before I wake, I pray the Lord my soul to take...."

According to a family friend attending the service, an emotional feeling came over this woman and those around her as the singers once again harmonized in the song, "Don't Weep for Me When I'm Gone." Marty seemed to be speaking through them to the congregation, urging his friends and family to celebrate his arrival in heaven.

As she quietly listened to the outpouring of love for her son, Joni rubbed her hand, still slightly numb from the frostbite earned in waving to the world from the apex of McKinley. She had hoped it would go away as the tissue and nerve endings started to heal. For now, though, a sense of numbness pervaded her whole life. The excitement was gone from it, but even this tragedy could not steal the memories of their climb of McKinley with her strong, vibrant twin sons.

Joni had found peace when standing at the top of the world, the sweetest, most amazing grace as she basked in the radiant moment. As Mike led the way, Marty had guided her there, knowing just the right words to safely direct her. Now Marty had gone on ahead, beyond the mountain top and into the heavens which had seemed just beyond her grasp. One day he would guide her the rest of the way into glory. For now she knew she was meant to keep living life to the fullest.

The weather experienced throughout the assault on McKinley was reported as the best in 30 years and that one four-day storm of a type which usually destroyed climbing teams, proved to be a blessing. Throughout her life and during the climb "angels of encouragement" had spurred her forward, letting her know she could succeed.

Having managed those triumphs, Joni tried to stand firm and be strong in her loss, staying focused on celebrating Marty's salvation, trusting that after a while God would restore her strength. "Thank you Lord that we can look forward to heaven and eternity together..... Remind us again tonight of the God of all grace who sustains his children. Help us as we wait before you tonight. Put your arms around each one of us and hold us close to you. Thank you for your love and your goodness to us. These things we pray in Jesus' name. Amen."

Had Marty or Mike perished before the historic climb of McKinley, it was apparent Joni would have never reached closer to the heavens and experienced, albeit vicariously, the view from the seldom reached window of the top of the world. This moving experience brought her in greater touch with her spirituality and peace within her self. Throughout the whole ordeal, there was not a thought of fame or fortune, just a quest for human dignity.

Joni overcame not only every pitfall on the 10,000-foot face the dangerous barrier of Mt. McKinley, but the equally important barriers of tradition and economics as she willed her dreams into reality. She inched her way to a world record with courage, skill and a competitive spirit. Her climb of self-discovery announced to the world that Joni Phelps was a competent, capable human being, an invincible optimist who just happened to be blind.

A new climb lay ahead, from the depths of grief. Centimeter by centimeter she would heal, finding her way as she recalled her moment of glory on the picturesque, bewitching, tantalizing, but perilous McKinley. When at the summit of the mountain on a clear day, most climbers could see only a hundred miles of beauty, but Joni through her special vision had envisioned the infinite reaches of God's playground, a spiritual regeneration.

This creative quilter and religious singer put the pieces of her life back together as she battled to regain the psychological wholeness akin to the multifaceted view that had galvanized her at the summit.

She came, she felt, she conquered, but what she conquered was not simply the topmost rock of North America's highest mountain, but the limits within herself.

An uphill challenge

The Calvary Singers

Photo by Barbara N. Ekey,   Copyright 1993

Shear Pleasure

Can I try it?

A new challenge -- training as a cyclist

About the Author

Barbara N. Ekey blends skills developed in nine years of teaching/writing in Denver, Minneapolis, Pennsylvania State University, Philadelphia and the New York City area as well as in Germany with her writing and photography, making it possible for her work to motivate individuals to overcome life's barriers. Outdoor adventures since childhood, a bachelor's degree from Iowa State University and a master's in educational psychology from the University of Minnesota lend added credibility to her books. While teaching for the Department of Defense in Wiesbaden, Germany, she received the D.O.D. Merit Teaching Award in 1970 for her creative skills in leading a diverse group of students to achieve success under her enthusiastic direction. She has worked as freelance photojournalist for Warren Times Observer, Erie Times-News, and other national newspapers & magazines, and is currently working on a sequel to her motivational children's book, "Catsup & Keys To Success."